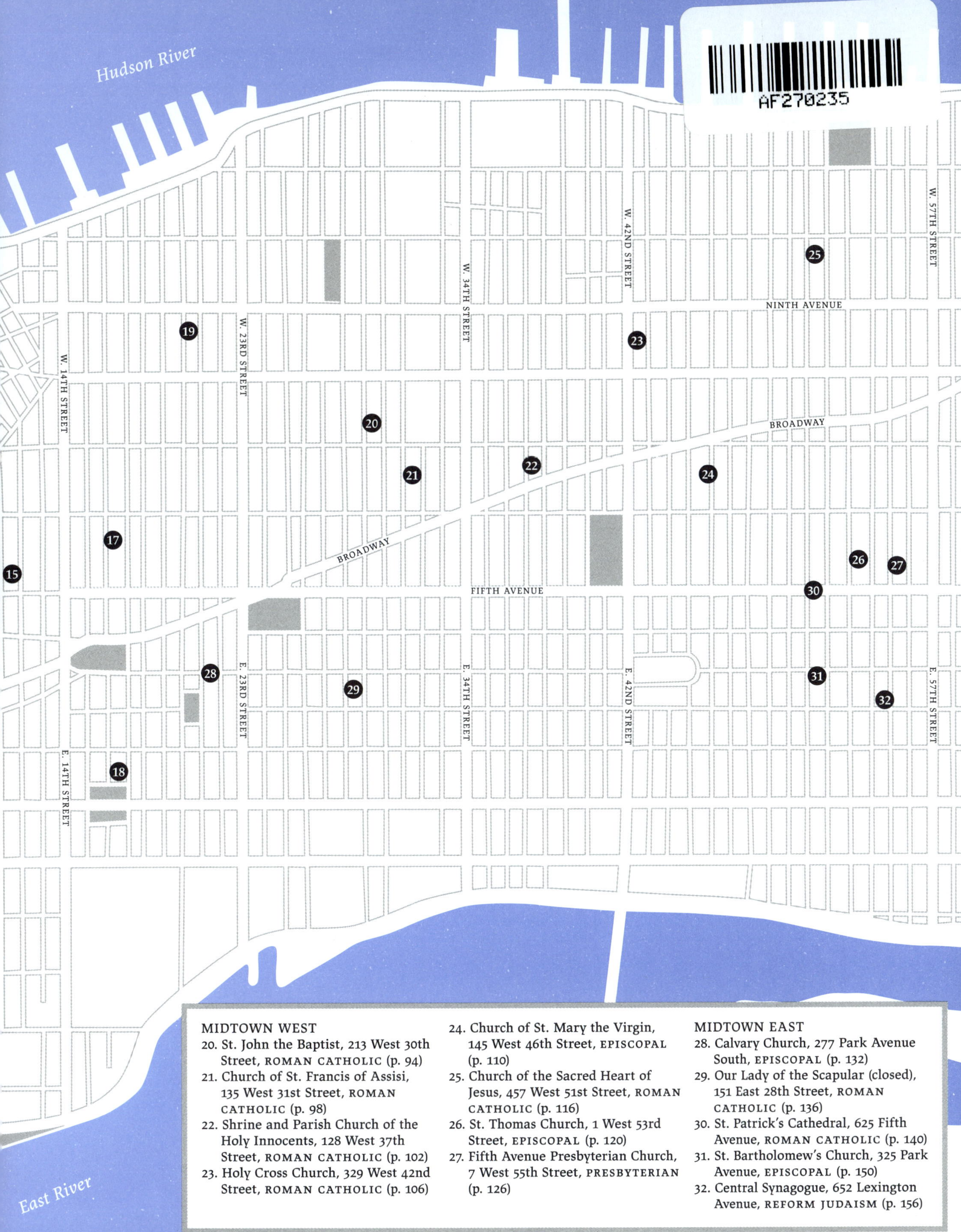

MIDTOWN WEST

20. St. John the Baptist, 213 West 30th Street, ROMAN CATHOLIC (p. 94)

21. Church of St. Francis of Assisi, 135 West 31st Street, ROMAN CATHOLIC (p. 98)

22. Shrine and Parish Church of the Holy Innocents, 128 West 37th Street, ROMAN CATHOLIC (p. 102)

23. Holy Cross Church, 329 West 42nd Street, ROMAN CATHOLIC (p. 106)

24. Church of St. Mary the Virgin, 145 West 46th Street, EPISCOPAL (p. 110)

25. Church of the Sacred Heart of Jesus, 457 West 51st Street, ROMAN CATHOLIC (p. 116)

26. St. Thomas Church, 1 West 53rd Street, EPISCOPAL (p. 120)

27. Fifth Avenue Presbyterian Church, 7 West 55th Street, PRESBYTERIAN (p. 126)

MIDTOWN EAST

28. Calvary Church, 277 Park Avenue South, EPISCOPAL (p. 132)

29. Our Lady of the Scapular (closed), 151 East 28th Street, ROMAN CATHOLIC (p. 136)

30. St. Patrick's Cathedral, 625 Fifth Avenue, ROMAN CATHOLIC (p. 140)

31. St. Bartholomew's Church, 325 Park Avenue, EPISCOPAL (p. 150)

32. Central Synagogue, 652 Lexington Avenue, REFORM JUDAISM (p. 156)

Divine New York

Divine New York

Inside the Historic Churches and
Synagogues of Manhattan

PHOTOGRAPHS BY
MICHAEL L. HOROWITZ

TEXT BY
ELIZABETH ANNE HARTMAN

ABBEVILLE PRESS PUBLISHERS

New York   London

Contents

FOREWORD 8
By Craig R. Whitney

PREFACE   10

LOWER MANHATTAN

Trinity Church   89 Broadway   14

John Street United Methodist Church   44 John Street   20

St. Paul's Chapel   209 Broadway   24

St. Peter's Church   22 Barclay Street   28

Church of the Transfiguration   29 Mott Street   32

Eldridge Street Synagogue   12 Eldridge Street   34

Shrine Church of the Most Precious Blood   113 Baxter Street   40

St. Mary Grand   440 Grand Street   42

Bialystoker Synagogue   7–11 Bialystoker Place   46

Kehila Kedosha Janina Synagogue and Museum
280 Broome Street   50

First Roumanian American Congregation (demolished)
89–93 Rivington Street   54

Basilica of St. Patrick's Old Cathedral   263 Mulberry Street   56

SOHO, GREENWICH VILLAGE, CHELSEA

St. Joseph's Church   371 Sixth Avenue   64

St. Nicholas of Myra Orthodox Church   288 East 10th Street   68

First Presbyterian Church   12 West 12th Street   72

Grace Church   802 Broadway   76

Church of St. Francis Xavier   46 West 16th Street   80

St. George's Church   209 East 16th Street   84

St. Peter's Episcopal Church   346 West 20th Street   88

MIDTOWN WEST

St. John the Baptist   213 West 30th Street   94

Church of St. Francis of Assisi   135 West 31st Street   98

Shrine and Parish Church of the Holy Innocents
128 West 37th Street   102

Holy Cross Church   329 West 42nd Street   106

Church of St. Mary the Virgin   145 West 46th Street   110

Church of the Sacred Heart of Jesus   457 West 51st Street   116

St. Thomas Church   1 West 53rd Street   120

Fifth Avenue Presbyterian Church   7 West 55th Street   126

MIDTOWN EAST

Calvary Church   277 Park Avenue South   132

Our Lady of the Scapular (closed)   151 East 28th Street   136

St. Patrick's Cathedral   625 Fifth Avenue   140

St. Bartholomew's Church   325 Park Avenue 150

Central Synagogue   652 Lexington Avenue   156

UPPER WEST SIDE

Church of St. Paul the Apostle   405 West 59th Street   164

Congregation Shearith Israel   8 West 70th Street   168

Church of the Blessed Sacrament   152 West 71st Street   172

West End Collegiate Church   245 West 77th Street   176

First Baptist Church   265 West 79th Street   178

Holy Trinity Catholic Church   213 West 82nd Street   182

Congregation Rodeph Sholom   7 West 83rd Street   186

B'nai Jeshurun   257 West 88th Street   190

Advent Lutheran Church   2504 Broadway   194

Holy Name of Jesus   207 West 96th Street   198

Ansche Chesed   251 West 100th Street   202

Church of the Ascension   221 West 107th Street 272   206

Cathedral of St. John the Divine
1047 Amsterdam Avenue   208

UPPER EAST SIDE

Central Presbyterian Church   593 Park Avenue   218

Temple Emanu-El   1 East 65th Street   220

Church of St. Vincent Ferrer   869 Lexington Avenue   226

Park East Synagogue   163 East 67th Street   230

St. John the Martyr (demolished)   250 East 72nd Street   234

Madison Avenue Presbyterian Church
921 Madison Avenue   236

Church of the Resurrection   119 East 74th Street   240

Archdiocesan Cathedral of the Holy Trinity
337 East 74th Street   242

St. Jean Baptiste Church   184 East 76th Street   246

Church of St. Monica   413 East 79th Street   250

St. Stephen of Hungary (closed)   414 East 82nd Street   254

Church of St. Ignatius Loyola   980 Park Avenue   256

St. Elizabeth of Hungary (closed)   211 East 83rd Street   260

Church of the Heavenly Rest   1085 Fifth Avenue   264

Our Lady of Good Counsel   230 East 90th Street   268

HARLEM

Salem United Methodist Church   211 West 129th Street   274

All Saints Church (closed)   47 East 129th Street   278

Mother African Methodist Episcopal Zion Church
140–148 West 137th Street   282

Abyssinian Baptist Church   132 Odell Clark Place   286

Church of the Intercession   550 West 155th Street   290

ACKNOWLEDGMENTS   296

RECOMMENDED READING   297

INDEX   298

PHOTO CREDITS   303

Foreword

What draws people to a church or a synagogue? There are the expected reasons—to pray, to worship, to celebrate, to mourn—but there can be unexpected ones as well. For some, it may be the beauty of Gothic arches and the vault they uphold, the detail of the stonework on the walls and columns, the plaques or paintings, the stained glass windows, the Ark and Torah scrolls. Or it could be the historical significance to the building or its connection with famous people, or simply the chance it provides to enjoy a few moments of quiet serenity. For others, it may just be a place to meet a friend outside, and it doesn't matter if the doors are open or closed.

It's when the doors are closed that Michael Horowitz is overcome by an urge: to get in and see what's inside. He has been feeling that compulsion since he was a child, and through a lifetime in photography and related fields, it has led him into sanctuaries the world over. This book shows what he has found inside scores of Christian and Jewish houses of worship over the years just in Manhattan, expertly explained in the text by Elizabeth Anne Hartman.

He started taking such photographs on a visit in 1994 to the Eldridge Street Synagogue in Lower Manhattan, a National Historic Landmark rescued from collapse in the 1980s. It was then beautifully restored to show what Jewish immigrants from Eastern Europe built in America a hundred years earlier to remind them of the culture they had come from. Another of Horowitz's early visits was to the Basilica of St. Patrick's Old Cathedral on Mulberry Street in Little Italy; it was built in the early nineteenth century for the immigrant Catholics, many of them Irish, who had come to the United States to escape famine and hardship at home. It was the Roman Catholic cathedral here for seventy years, until the completion of the new St. Patrick's Cathedral on Fifth Avenue became the seat of the archdiocese in 1879.

Not all the buildings in this book are that old, but do not expect to find modernistic ones—those that inspire him were all designed and/or built before about 1935. Some are famous; some you may not know at all. Mainstream churches in New York have been losing parishioners in recent years, and one Roman Catholic church he photographed for this collection—All Saints on East 129th Street, designed by James Renwick Jr., who also did St. Patrick's Cathedral on Fifth Avenue—was later deconsecrated in 2017. Designated a landmark by the city, the exterior will survive, but the interior is no more. Fortunately, it is immortalized in the photographs in this book. Another church, St. John the Martyr on East 72nd Street, was not spared after its deconsecration. Demolished, the church only remains in the hearts of former parishioners—and in this book as well.

I first met Michael Horowitz in a church in Brooklyn I belong to that is not included in this collection. I am often there just to practice the organ, which I did while Michael was busily taking photographs of the sanctuary from end to end and top to bottom. Playing the organ has been one of my reasons for going inside many of the buildings in this book, too. For example, one of the largest church buildings in the world, the Episcopal Cathedral of St. John the Divine on Amsterdam Avenue in Morningside Heights—601 feet from end to end, big enough to hold a herd of animals every October 4 to be blessed on the feast of St. Francis of Assisi—also holds one of the largest and most glorious pipe organs in the city. Many kinds of music are at home there, and most notably Duke Ellington's funeral took place there in 1974. The chances of hearing great music are high in many of the places you find in this book. St. Thomas Church, nearly opposite St. Patrick's on Fifth Avenue, has had famous organists and choirmasters over the decades and also has a choir school. High-Medieval atmosphere with Gregorian chant and incense also draws many to St. Mary the Virgin, just off Times Square at 145 East 46th Street.

Additionally, places of worship help shape our culture and history. Temple Emanu-El, which, at Fifth Avenue and 65th Street, is as big as a cathedral, was founded a few buildings earlier in 1845 as the first Reform congregation in New York City, and today has thousands of members and a museum of more than a thousand examples of Judaic history to see. Many notables of New York City have been members, including Lyman Bloomingdale and Michael Bloomberg, to mention just two.

The Abyssinian Baptist Church on West 138th Street in Harlem—between Lenox Avenue and Adam Clayton Powell Jr. Boulevard, named after one of its pastors—is a vibrant center of African American cultural and community life. The largest Baptist congregation in the city, it got its start in Lower Manhattan in 1808, when sixteen Black members of another church there walked out in protest against racially segregated seating. The new congregation moved around the island over the years, but by the early twentieth century, Reverend Dr. Powell Sr., an inspiring preacher, had attracted thousands of members. The present imposing edifice housing the church went up in the early 1920s. Adam Clayton Powell Jr. later succeeded his father as pastor, and in 1945 was elected as the first Black congressman from the city, serving fourteen terms in Washington before retiring in 1971. Fats Waller, whose father was another one of the church's ministers, was one of its organists; and Nat King Cole was married there in 1948. The Abyssinian congregation has supported numerous projects for housing and community development, including the building of a new high school nearby, the Thurgood Marshall Academy for Learning and Social Change, in 1993. The church also provides help for poor people in Ethiopia—known as Abyssinia in biblical times.

In sum, *Divine New York* is a splendid collection of monuments of faith, art, history, and cultural diversity in this one borough of America's largest city. Feel free to be inspired by the riches Michael Horowitz and Elizabeth Hartman show you here. Go see some of them yourself, if you can!

CRAIG R. WHITNEY

Preface

An 1853 article in Putnam's Monthly Magazine of American Literature, Science and Art, said, "New York is proud of her Churches, and she well may be, as the forest of spires seen above the roof of the level lines of houses indicated, as plainly as the forest of masts at the wharves, her thrift and greatness." While those spires are now dwarfed by the city's towering skyscrapers, New York can still take pride in its panoply of houses of worship from cathedrals to humble churches, from synagogues to mosques. There are thousands in the city and almost every one in Manhattan "is worthy of a story and an affectionate description."

It would be impossible to discuss them all and even more impossible to photograph all of them. Michael Horowitz has been photographing churches—well, everything really—since his grandparents gave him a Kodak Brownie Holiday camera when he was five years old. So we set parameters. The houses of worship explored in these pages are all in the borough of Manhattan and were built between 1698 and 1935, when the Depression and the imminent war more or less put a halt to the grand architectural building in the city. These chronological bounds also necessarily limit our survey to Christian churches and Jewish synagogues.

Further limiting the criteria was our agreement to include only those houses of worship whose interiors were aesthetically beautiful *and* had an interesting history. Many sacred spaces that would have qualified no longer exist. In fact, some of the buildings featured in this book have been demolished or decommissioned from religious use. Fortunately, Michael was able to capture the splendor of these before they disappeared. Those that fit into this category are noted as such.

A far more extensive overview is to be found in David W. Dunlap's *From Abyssinian to Zion: A Guide to Manhattan's Houses of Worship*. He has compiled snapshot histories of hundreds of places of worship, old and new, here and gone. This book could not have been written without the foundation his book provides. He is quoted often in the following pages.

The history of places of worship in New York City is the history of immigration. The waves of immigrants who poured into the city were looking not only for a place to worship in the customs and rituals of their homelands, but also for solace, community, and hope that they could experience the American dream and pull themselves out of desperate poverty and wretched tenements. Sanctuaries were as much home to religious activity as they were to social events, community service, and political activism.

Observing the growth and movement of congregations from small makeshift spaces in rented rooms and buildings, to private homes, and then to increasingly larger and grander structures reveals the extraordinary successes—and failures—of New York's great experiment as a melting pot. The nativists, with support from the Know-Nothing political party, deplored immigrants. In early New York, anti-Catholic laws prevented Catholics from worshipping publicly. The same was true even earlier—when the Spanish and Portuguese Jews arrived in New Amsterdam, they were forbidden to worship publicly. When the Italians came to our shores, the Irish who had previously immigrated relegated them to the basements of the sanctuaries. Blacks were banned from some houses of worship, and in others they had to sit separately and take communion after all the white parishioners—even after the children.

Of course, there was also much kindness, as illustrated by churches opening their doors to other congregations—including Jewish ones—in times of need. Some of the houses of worship over the years were home to myriad religions and denominations.

After immigration came a migration. As Lower Manhattan became more and more crowded, and as the poor began to prosper, there was a gradual but definitive shift uptown. To remain vital, many congregations were forced to follow their flocks, which meant heading north.

Some churches and synagogues were built quickly and went from concept to reality in a straightforward timeline. Others would lay a cornerstone and wait years, if not decades, for the walls to be erected. And before their sanctuaries were built, congregations were formed in barns, in lofts, in living rooms, and in delis. All this makes declaring a single origin date nearly impossible; and much of this chronology is lost to history. For some, the founding date and the laying of the cornerstone is known; for others, the date of dedication is known or the date that the sanctuary was open for worship—oftentimes before construction was completed. Thus, there is no single date attached to a particular church, but rather several important ones.

Each sacred space is a microcosm of the struggle of immigrants, the power of wealth, the need for community, and the human desire to seek spiritual guidance. These spaces give us the privilege of experiencing the great evolution of the majestic island of Manhattan in all its glory and all its pain.

ELIZABETH ANNE HARTMAN
MICHAEL L. HOROWITZ
February 2021

Lower Manhattan

Trinity Church

89 Broadway

The First Church

EPISCOPAL
CORNERSTONE LAID 1841

Trinity Church today is the third incarnation of the first Anglican church on Manhattan Island. In 1696, New York boasted a population of four thousand, which, even then, represented a rather heterogeneous group. Twelve Anglican men of the four thousand purchased land from the Lutherans for twenty pounds with the approval of Governor Benjamin Fletcher, who had established Anglicanism as the official religion of New York. On May 6, 1697, the Anglican parish received its charter from King William III of England accompanied by a land grant that stipulated an annual rent of one peppercorn due to the English Crown.

The first of Trinity's churches was built in 1698. Its inaugural rector and the bishop of London, William Vesey, conducted the church's first services on March 13, 1698, in what was, as David W. Dunlap describes in *From Abyssinian to Zion*, a "barn-like" structure. Throughout the 1700s, Trinity's steeple and belfry were the highest points in New York, and the church became the "it" place to be to (literally) ring out the old and ring in a new year. Even today, the bells of Trinity remain a venerable part of its history. In 2009, a set of twelve bells was installed, making it the only church in the nation with that many.

The Great Fire of 1776 destroyed the original Trinity edifice, which was ignited by Revolutionary War battles in Manhattan. Construction of the second church had to wait until the end of the war; it didn't begin until 1788 and was completed in 1790. While Trinity was still under construction, a monumental event happened when on April 30, 1789, George Washington was inaugurated as the first president of the United States. After the official ceremony concluded, Washington went to St. Paul's Chapel for a memorial service of thanksgiving, officiated by the rector of Trinity. Less than a year later, when the new Trinity Church was consecrated, Washington attended the service, and worshipped there until the capital was moved to Philadelphia.

The New York winter of 1838 to 1839 was a particularly nasty one. Heavy snows caused the roof of the second Trinity Church to sink, and an investigation showed that the structure was in danger of collapse. It was demolished in 1839, having stood for only about half as long as the original. By this time, as Clifford P. Morehouse posits in his book *Trinity: Mother of All Churches,* "Trinity was no longer a comfortable, closely knit parish church, but a Christian outpost in a migratory and constantly shifting population of differing religious and national backgrounds." Also by now, New York wasn't a scruffy diamond in the rough; its sparkling gems were revealed by its luxurious hotels, grand theaters, and posh stores. A humble rectangle would no longer do for what was arguably the largest, most influential, and wealthiest Episcopal parish in New York, if not the country.

The architect Richard Upjohn, a British émigré whose reputation was growing in the States, was selected to draw up plans and supervise the erection of the church. His design was influenced by the ecclesiological movement, an English-inspired type of architecture for churches that, according to Catherine W. Bishir, "promoted 'authentic' medieval forms to inspire worship in keeping with the values of the middle ages." Upjohn did not adhere strictly to this movement's mandates, but he did incorporate some of its principles for Trinity, particularly in the beauty and purity of its Perpendicular Gothic style (an emphasis on strong verticals) for which it is renowned. His plans also included a much deeper chancel than what was customary, the chancel being very important to the movement. The brownstone of the exterior fulfills the ecclesiological dictum to use natural materials.

Stained glass windows were uncommon in Protestant churches during this period, and there was a dearth of trained artisans to construct them. Upjohn overcame this obstacle by learning how to design the chancel windows himself. "Trinity's design was revolutionary," Judith Dupré writes in *Churches.* She adds: "One of the earliest and finest examples of the Gothic Revival in America, its monumental size, soaring verticality, and abundant decorative detail introduced the Gothic Style to Manhattan and so to the rest of America."

Beyond having a master architect, Trinity has benefited greatly by being the recipient of bounteous donations from its wealthy patrons, one of whom was John Jacob Astor, whose father, William B. Astor, left him $20 million when he died in 1875. John Jacob had been a vestryman of Trinity for ten years by this time. He and his brother, William Astor, erected a magnificent altar made of marble and a reredos of stone for the church as a memorial to their father. The main part of the reredos that spans nearly the whole width (35 ft./10.7 m) of the chancel is constructed of Caen stone with elaborate carvings of the twelve apostles. Beneath the reredos is the eleven-foot altar made of pure white statuary marble. A superaltar is comprised of red Lisbon marble, with the words "Holy, Holy, Holy" inlaid in mosaics. In *New York 1880,* Robert M. Stern says that "known collectively as the Astor Memorial, these elements provided Trinity Church with a focus on a scale of magnificence hitherto absent in any American church."

The magnanimity continued into the next generation. When John Jacob died, his son, William Waldorf Astor, gave a contribution in the form of imposing, exquisitely sculpted bronze doors, designed by Richard M. Hunt, that provide an entrance from the Broadway side of the building. Carved by Austrian sculptor Karl Bitter, the doors recall Lorenzo Ghiberti's *Gates of Paradise* for the Baptistery of St. John in Florence.

     LOWER MANHATTAN

Fit for royalty, Trinity was visited by members of the royal family, including a young Prince of Wales in 1860 who was later crowned King Edward VII. Fifty-nine years later, the far more notorious King Edward VIII, who abdicated the throne, sat in the same pew that his grandfather had occupied.

The graveyard, too, hosts boldface names. The best known is Alexander Hamilton, a founding father and first secretary whose fame has been renewed since the blockbuster musical *Hamilton* stormed popular culture. Both he and his wife, Eliza, worshipped there, and both are buried in the adjacent graveyard. Also interred there is the inventor of the steamboat, Robert Fulton, and the founder of New York University, Albert Gallatin.

For more than three hundred years, the parish of Trinity Church has stood on the same plot of land (albeit with three different roofs and walls) and prevailed throughout the tribulations of wars, fire, the Great Depression, and most recently, that apocalyptic day, 9/11. Indeed, on that day, the church offered what may have been the first institutional response just after the second plane hit, according to David Dunlap. As people streamed into the church for shelter and solace, an impromptu service commenced. During the singing of the hymn "O God, Our Help in Ages Past," "there came the thunderous collapse of the South Tower, casting the church into Stygian pitch and ash," Dunlap described. In the weeks and months following, Trinity became a resource for essential services, food, rest, and comfort for first responders and throngs of others.

John Street United Methodist Church

44 John Street

"The Mother Church of American Methodism"

METHODIST
CORNERSTONE LAID 1841

OPPOSITE
View from the balcony of the sanctuary and altar with its characteristically austere Methodist decor

The establishment of the John Street United Methodist Church, which celebrated its 250th anniversary in 2016, goes back to the very roots of Methodism. Philip Embury, a local preacher for John Wesley (Methodism's founder); his wife; and his cousin Barbara Ruckle immigrated to New York in 1760. Some of their fellow Methodists—to Barbara Heck's great distress—were drifting from Wesley's teachings. Heck exhorted her cousin to act: "Philip, you must preach to us or we shall all go to hell!" Embury obliged and began conducting services in his home, and participation grew quickly. In 1768, the congregation purchased two lots on John Street where the first building, Wesley Chapel, was dedicated on October 30 of that year, making it the first permanent home of America's oldest continuous congregation.

In 1817 the original plain barn with its blue stucco exterior was replaced by a larger structure, which caused the first rift in New York's Methodist community. The interior boasted plush carpets and ornate decor, appalling congregants who upheld the traditional austere Methodist approach to materiality, and left to form a rival church about a half mile north on Chrystie Street. Later, in 1839, when a fire ravaged the 1817 building, it was torn down and replaced in 1841 with the Greek Revival style church that stands today. But this time opulence was absent. The simple interior seen today is much like it was more than a century and a half ago, with pews made of Santo Domingo mahogany. Displayed on the sanctuary walls are tablets dedicated to the memory of Philip Embury, Barbara Heck, and other Methodist pioneers.

The decision to rebuild on the same site caused quite an uproar. Those who wanted to stay on John Street respected the church's history as the cradle of Methodism, while the proponents for the uptown move wanted it in a convenient

HYMNS
698
364
159
139
IN REMEMBRANCE OF ME

neighborhood. The acrimony between the two factions came to a head with a street brawl. The history buffs won but had to rebuild the membership after losing many to the embarrassing brouhaha.

Well before the Civil War, the church took an active role in social justice. Church member and slave Peter Williams, who had been owned by a British Loyalist who fled back to England after the Revolutionary War, feared that he would be sold at the auction block, so Wesley Chapel bought and freed him in 1784. In 1796, Williams and one of the Black deacons seceded to form the country's first all-Black Methodist congregation, the African Methodist Episcopal Zion Church.

Many well-known names have graced these pews. Among them was Sojourner Truth, who was a member, the church being an early advocate for the abolition movement. John Street was home to a diverse population of Black men and women—including slaves—and it welcomed Black preachers and deacons, although Blacks and whites were not permitted to sit together. Another boldface name is James Harper, who was mayor of New York in 1844–45 and the founder of Harper & Brothers publishing company in 1825.

St. Paul's Chapel

209 Broadway

"The Little Chapel That Stood"

EPISCOPAL
CORNERSTONE LAID 1764

In the New York Landmarks Conservancy's Tourist in Your Own Town series, the narration about St. Paul's Chapel suggests that there is no better example than this chapel for why we save our architectural heritage. Indeed. Beyond the fact that it is the only extant prerevolutionary-period building in Manhattan, it has been host to both highly orchestrated and shockingly unplanned watershed events in US history.

From 1764 to 1766, St. Paul's Chapel was built for the convenience of Episcopalians (then still members of the Church of England) who, living in rural farmhouses spread out among the wheatfields of the area, didn't want to make the trek over fields and unpaved roads to Trinity Church about a quarter-mile south. Trinity was built first and is the oldest parish in the city, but after the church building was decimated by the Great Fire of 1776, it ceded the honor of being the oldest prerevolutionary structure to St. Paul's.

There is some doubt as to who is responsible for the design of the Georgian (Colonial) style church. According to David Dunlap, Thomas McBean is most often credited as the architect, but recent scholarship shows the hand of Andrew Gautier. Dunlap also proffers that "it seems to have been patterned on St. Martin-in-the-Fields" in London. But the brownstone building material is strictly homegrown, composed of Manhattan schist.

St. Paul's first momentous event occurred on April 30, 1789, the day when General George Washington was inaugurated and became the first president of the United States. Following the ceremony, because Trinity was not yet rebuilt after the fire, he processed to St. Paul's to offer thanksgiving prayers in the sanctuary, which was filled with members of both Houses of Congress. Its tasteful, minimally adorned interior befitted a man who refused to be crowned king. Until the capital

The organ and loft rise opposite the altar, where one of the fourteen Waterford chandeliers can also be seen.

moved to Philadelphia, President Washington continued to worship in his reserved presidential pew. Another president, George H. W. Bush, sat in the same pew to mark the bicentennial of Washington's inauguration.

On September 11, 2001, when the World Trade Center was attacked and the towers fell, the chapel remained standing even while three feet of debris buried the churchyard. Hence, "The Little Chapel That Stood." Not only did St. Paul's miraculously avoid damage, but its sanctuary became a very different sacred space as it provided shelter and comfort to the firefighters, police officers, and other rescue and recovery teams. Exhausted physically, emotionally, and spiritually, they stumbled in twenty-four hours a day for the warmth, food, fresh socks, and spiritual succor—President Washington's pew became a podiatrist center. According to a *New York Times* article by Dunlap, volunteer and 9/11 widow Fiona Havlish said, "It was like walking into pure love. I didn't consider it a church. It was a sanctuary."

In the days following the initial crisis, St. Paul's—both inside and out—became a de facto memorial. Its comfortingly sturdy and solid iron fence became the place where people left missing-persons posters, photographs, flowers, poems, and other miscellany that paid homage and offered hope for the thousands of the missing.

Later on the first anniversary of the attack, St. Paul's became home to an exhibit, Out of the Dust, a display about its Ground Zero ministry. It was intended to remain on display for three months but it quickly drew crowds that grew and grew. By March 2004, a million visitors had come to the sanctuary to view the display. In April 2004, a new exhibition was installed, Unwavering Spirit: Hope and Healing at Ground Zero, that included panels around the churchyard illustrating the history of the church and, inside, deliberately ephemeral and movable display stations. Audio and video clips at the display stations told stories from those who volunteered and others who gave and received messages of hope.

View of the original boxed pews prior to the renovation in the 1990s. The pews were removed after 9/11 to meet the postcrisis needs of the rescue community.

Original architectural monuments and details still remain. Among them is the Montgomery Monument on the east porch of the church facing Broadway. It honors General Richard Montgomery, an eminent Revolutionary War officer who was killed in combat in Quebec in 1775. Believed to be the first Revolutionary War monument commissioned by the Continental Congress, it was sculpted of marble by Jean-Jacques Caffieri. In 1794, a wooden steeple was added to the exterior.

Inside is an altarpiece, the *Glory*, which depicts clouds and lightning enveloping Mt. Sinai, symbolizing God's glory and the giving of the Ten Commandments to the Israelites, from Exodus 24. Architect Pierre L'Enfant, who planned the layout of Washington, DC, designed the work. Illuminating the sanctuary are fourteen original hand-cut glass chandeliers from Waterford, Ireland, installed in 1802. And above Washington's pew, most fittingly, is an eighteenth-century painting of the Great Seal of the United States of America. It was commissioned by the vestry of Trinity Church in 1785 and is one of the earliest known depictions of the seal that was adopted by Congress in 1782.

Today, St. Paul's Chapel welcomes all. In addition to its Episcopalian services, it holds many interfaith worship events and has been the home for the worship services of Tamid: The Downtown Synagogue since 2012.

St. Peter's Church

22 Barclay Street

The First Catholic Church
in New York City

ROMAN CATHOLIC
CORNERSTONE LAID 1836

Established in 1785, and still located on its original site, St. Peter's Church is the first and oldest Catholic church in New York City. It was organized only two years after the end of the Revolutionary War and five years before the present US government was formed. While so many churches founded later tended to be born out of either divisiveness or a yearning to minister to a particular ethnic group, St. Peter's was not. At the time of its founding, there were only four hundred Catholics in New York, all immigrants but not all from the same place—some were French, others Spanish or Irish.

In the seventeenth and eighteenth centuries, the Catholic population of New York was minuscule—in 1643, the French Jesuit missionary Isaac Jogues visited New Amsterdam and found only *two* Catholics. But when the influx of immigrants began to flow in the eighteenth century, so did the growth of the Catholic population, which did not sit well with the overwhelmingly Protestant city. In fact, until 1784, the city was virulently anti-Catholic. But in 1784, with the Catholic population's exponential growth, the discriminatory laws were repealed. A year later, the Catholic Church was incorporated in the city of New York, and through the efforts of a group of men under the leadership of the French consul, Hector St. John de Crèvecœur, and the Spanish ambassador, Don Diego de Gardoqui, St. Peter's was founded.

At the same time, New York served as the capital of the new nation and became a crossroads for foreign ambassadors and businessmen, some of whom were Catholic, including several members of Congress. A small group of city residents met privately at the home of the Spanish ambassador to attend mass. As the group grew, they embarked on a plan to build a church with the counsel of Father Whelan, a member of the Capuchin Order of Ireland. Whelan suggested that the pastor would

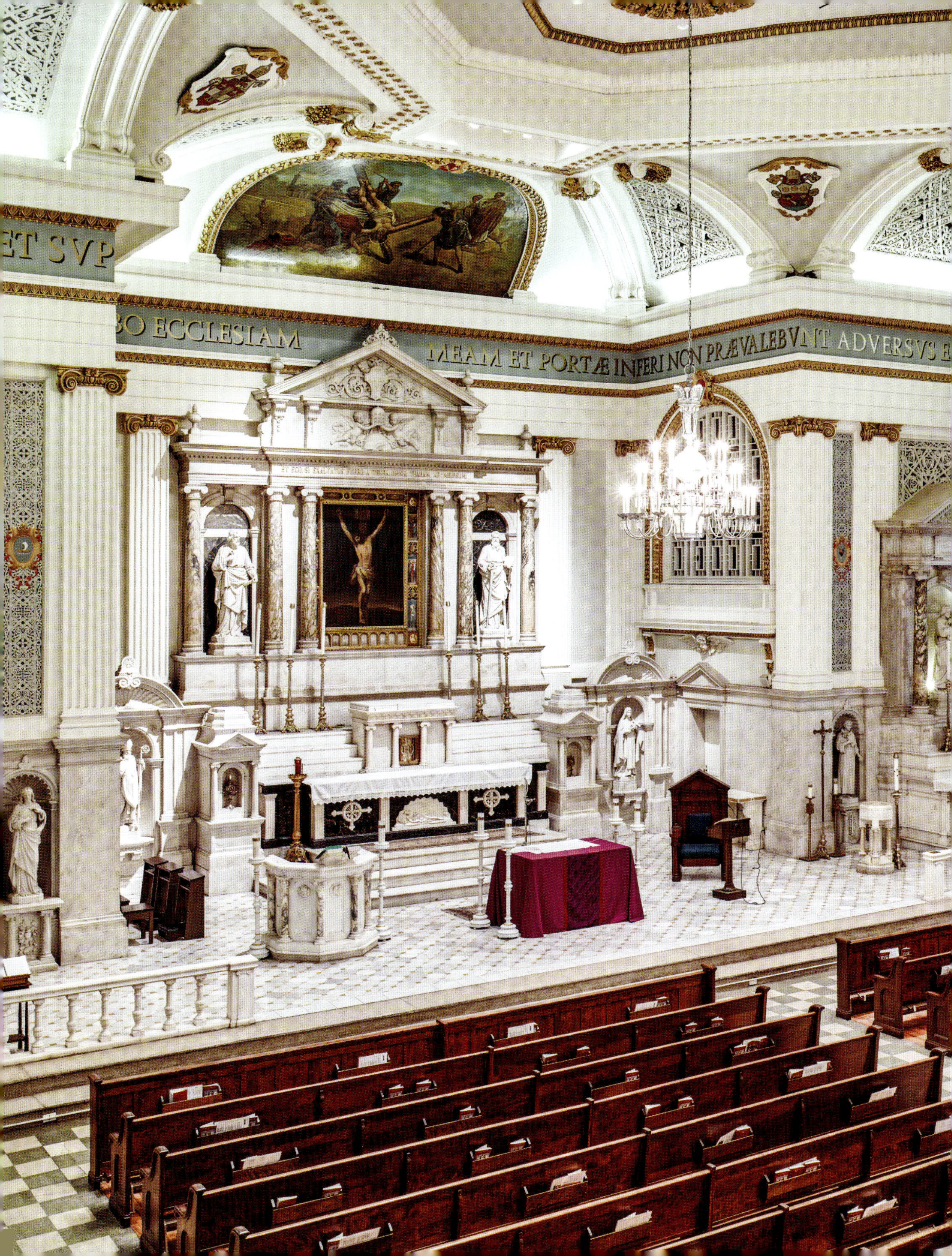

In the center beneath the intricately carved pediment is Crucifixion, *a painting by a Mexican artist, José Vallejo, a gift from the archbishop of Mexico City.*

need to know at least six languages spoken by various members of the congregation: English, French, German, Spanish, Portuguese, and Irish.

The Protestant Corporation of Trinity Church responded with an agreement to lease some of their land known as "the Farm of Trinity Church." This is the site at the corner of Barclay and Church where St. Peter's still stands today. With Ambassador De Gardoqui presiding over the ceremony, the cornerstone was laid on October 5, 1785. In the cornerstone, the ambassador placed Spanish coins minted during the reign of King Charles III. More coins from Spain helped support building the church when, in the following spring of 1786, King Charles III donated a thousand silver dollars. With the help of other donations, the first church opened for mass on November 4, 1786.

In 1836, the ceiling of the original church collapsed, and by this time, the building couldn't accommodate the growing number of worshippers; some had to stand outside to hear mass. Plans were made to build a bigger church and the cornerstone for the new Greek Revival structure, designed by John R. Haggerty and Thomas Thomas, was laid in 1836. The official consecration for the church—now debt free—took place in 1885, one hundred years after its original founding. By 1893 the parish had twenty thousand congregants.

In 1800, a time when there were no public schools in New York City, St. Peter's opened the doors of its free Catholic school for primary education. It laid the groundwork for today's diocesan system of parish schools. By 1874, the school had 1,810 students.

Among its venerable members were Félix Varela y Morales, a Cuban priest who fought for independence, was exiled in New York, and became vicar general of the Catholic Archdiocese in New York, and Pierre Toussaint. The latter is on a path to be canonized, which would make him the first African American saint. A member of St. Peter's for sixty-six years, he was born a slave in Haiti circa 1766, where he worked for the Bérard family, wealthy owners of a sugarcane plantation. When slave rebellions broke out around 1793, the family came to New York, thinking that they would ride out the unrest and then return home. But their stay became permanent when their plantation was burned to the ground. Shortly after their move, Monsieur Bérard died and the family was left with nothing and no source of income—except for Toussaint.

In New York, Toussaint had been training to be a hairdresser—no small feat with elaborate hairstyles stacked high and adorned with curls and intricately styled ribbons. Working long days and nights, Toussaint became the Vidal Sassoon of the late eighteenth to early nineteenth centuries in New York, attending to elites such as the niece of Alexander Hamilton and Mrs. Caroline Schermerhorn Astor. He was able—and willing—to support the Bérard family. Upon her death, Madame Bérard allowed Toussaint to buy his freedom, at which point he married but continued to support the family. He became one of the city's most prominent philanthropists.

Inside the church over the main altar is a painting of the Crucifixion by a Mexican artist, José Vallejo, a gift from Núñez de Haro, the archbishop of Mexico City, in 1789. The stained glass windows are of Renaissance style. The pews that line the nave, originally installed in 1840, are made of wood from trees that grew along the Hudson River. They were recently restored to their former burnished splendor.

Like other downtown churches, St. Peter's played a sacred role in the wake of the 9/11 attack. The body of Reverend Mychal F. Judge, officially the first casualty at the World Trade Center, was brought to St. Peter's by firefighters and laid before the altar. In the sanctuary, Father Madigan had these words of Christ inscribed in gold leaf: *Tu es Petrus, et hanc super Petramaedificabo Ecclesiam meam. Et portae inferi non praevalebunt adversus eam.* ("You are Peter, and upon this rock I will build my Church. And the gates of hell will not prevail against it.")

Church of the Transfiguration

29 Mott Street

"The Church of the Immigrants"

ROMAN CATHOLIC
BUILT 1801

Cuban priest Félix Varela y Morales (1788–1853) supported the country's independence from Spain and thus was a political exile in New York, where he became a member of St. Peter's Church. In 1827, he founded Transfiguration Church and later purchased Christ Protestant Episcopal Church on Ann Street. The parish landed at its present site on Mott Street in 1853. After Father Varela retired, Bishop John Hughes purchased the church on Mott Street from Zion Episcopal Church—the building was affordable because its prior owners had given up on resuscitating the neighborhood, which was part of the notoriously violent Five Points area.

The stone Georgian-Gothic building was erected in 1801 with schist from a local quarry and walls thirty inches thick. In 1868, architect Henry Engelbert, who had just completed the rebuilding of Old St. Patrick's Cathedral on Mulberry Street, designed additions to the church, including its green bell tower. Four columns of mottled red Vermont marble support the chapel. The New York City Landmarks Preservation Commission called it "one of the finest ecclesiastical buildings of its time."

The first group of immigrants to whom Father Varela ministered were Irish, but as they assimilated, the congregation became predominantly Italian. Yet, the Irish leaders of the church forbade the Italians to worship in the main sanctuary and relegated them to the basement. It wasn't until 1902 when Reverend Ernest Coppo became pastor that Italians were allowed upstairs, and by this time waves of Chinese immigrants dominated the local landscape. This group, too, faced ugly discrimination—but within a few years a Chinese pastor, who had done missionary work, was brought into the fold. By the 1940s, the Maryknoll Fathers, respected for their missionary work in China, managed the church, and a Chinese school was established. Today, at Transfiguration, services are held in English, Cantonese, and Mandarin. The largest Chinese Catholic church in the country, it is known as "The Church of the Immigrants."

Eldridge Street Synagogue

12 Eldridge Street

Longest Continuous Restoration
of a Synagogue

ORTHODOX JUDAISM
DEDICATED 1887

What do the banker Sender Jarmulowsky, entertainers Eddie Cantor and Al Jolson, artist Ben Shahn, scientist Jonas Salk, Nobel Prize–winner Linus Pauling, and actors Sam Jaffe and Edward Robinson have in common? They were all at one time or another members of the Eldridge Street Synagogue.

The arc of this storied synagogue is one of a stupendous rise and fall in tandem with waxing and waning waves of immigration. The story begins in 1852 when a small group of Polish and Russian immigrants met in a space on the Lower East Side and called their congregation Beth Hamedrash (House of Study). It was the first synagogue in the United States to have trained rabbis to perform ritual functions and interpret Jewish law. Right from the start, it distinguished itself from other synagogues by welcoming Jews from all over Eastern Europe while other congregations were defined by the towns or cities from which they came. It was also economically diverse; migrants right off the boat, peddlers, sweatshop workers, bankers, and entertainers were among its members.

In 1878, just ahead of a massive wave of immigrants who were about to begin their odyssey over the Atlantic and through Ellis Island, Beth Hamedrash merged with the congregation Holkhe Yosher Vizaner and two years later the united synagogue officially changed its name to Khal Adas Jeshurun (Community of the People of Israel). By 1887, the flood of immigrants had become a tsunami. From 1880 to 1924, more than twenty-five million immigrants, including more than two and a half million Jews, came to the country. Although there were other ports of entry, approximately 85 percent of Jewish immigrants from Eastern Europe came to New York, and of those roughly 75 percent settled on the Lower East Side—an astonishing figure that illuminates how the Lower East Side became the most densely populated Jewish community in the world.

34

With the congregation's population bursting—and flourishing—Khal Adas Jeshurun built a glorious building at 12 Eldridge Street, making it the first synagogue that was erected specifically as a Jewish house of worship and thereafter familiarly known as the Eldridge Street Synagogue. Although other congregations existed—and were also thriving—they still were housed in structures that had been adapted from storefronts, event halls, and even former churches. While most of the city's synagogues served Reform congregations, Eldridge remained "almost defiantly Orthodox and decidedly Eastern European," as Gerard R. Wolfe describes in *The Synagogues of New York's Lower East Side*.

The brothers Peter and Francis William Herter were the architects of the structure that Joseph Berger, in his foreword to Wolfe's book, calls "a marvelous pastiche of Moorish, Gothic, and Romanesque styles." Wolfe cautions us not to confuse the pair of brothers with an entirely different duo, Gustave and Christian Herter, who were interior designers for the opulent mansions for the crème de la crème of the Gilded Age. Quite the opposite, Peter and Francis were known for building tenement buildings of better quality and more embellishment than most. Many of the motifs that they incorporated into Eldridge Street, such as Stars of David and horseshoe arches, can be found in some of the tenements they built as well. They were also known for designing buildings with grand facades, and the Eldridge Street Synagogue was no exception with a stunning stained glass rose window, Moorish windows, and elaborate roof finials.

The main sanctuary had more than three thousand square feet with a central dome fifty feet high and seating for 750 worshippers and was surrounded by dozens of stained glass windows. Its surfaces were lavishly decorated with celestial patterns adorning the walls, so ascending to the balcony one feels as if they are truly reaching for the stars. Victorian glass lampshades and a grand chandelier provided light that bounced off the highly polished oak pews and silver adornments. Trompe l'oeil murals of textile hangings bookended the ark. For Emma Lazarus's poor, tired, huddled masses and wretched refuse, leaving the smelly, grimy, crowded streets behind and passing through the magnificent facade offered not only a spiritual sanctuary, but also a respite in Arcadian splendor.

For fifty years the synagogue thrived with thousands of worshippers sitting on the highly polished wooden pews. In 1924 the country introduced Immigrant Quota

Laws that sharply reduced the number of Jews coming to the Lower East Side. The population was further eroded by people moving to the outer boroughs and the congregation's members dwindled steadily. In 1940, the dearth of members was such that they could no longer afford to maintain the main sanctuary and the doors were closed. A small group continued to attend Sabbath services, but in a smaller space below the grand sanctuary.

By the 1970s the building was on the verge of collapse. In 1971, Wolfe, the author, architectural historian, and former professor at NYU, brought a group of his students to visit the synagogue. The crumbling state of decay moved the students to unanimously agree that something had to be done. Wolfe organized an informal group, the Synagogue Rescue Project, to assess priorities in restoring the building, and the group decided that repairing electricity and heat and a Band-Aid measure to fix the worst roof leaks were essential. They also sought—and won—its designation as a New York City Landmark in 1980. In 1996, it was designated a National Historic Landmark.

OPPOSITE and ABOVE Artist Kiki Smith's radiant stained glass window illuminates the pastiche of Moorish, Gothic, and Romanesque styles.

What became clear was that this ad hoc group didn't have the resources to oversee the massive restoration demands. Serendipity put them in contact with Roberta Brandes Gratz, a journalist and urban critic with an impressive record of historic preservation. In 1986 Gratz founded the Eldridge Street Project as a nonsectarian, not-for-profit organization with the mission to preserve and reinterpret the role of the majestic building. In 2007, twenty years and $20 million later, the restoration was completed and a new entity was born: the Eldridge Street Synagogue and Museum, with the distinction of being called in the *New Yorker* the "Longest Time for Continuous Restoration, Synagogue."

The trompe l'oeil murals were restored. The layers of dirt and debris on the pews, the tarnish on the silver, and the inches-thick dust on the Victorian lampshades were all removed, and the magnificence of the decor renewed. The enormous, elegant Victorian chandelier, once illuminated with gas flames, was refurbished.

One important architectural design element was still missing though. The magnificent stained glass rose window that adorned the east end of the building was destroyed in the great hurricane of 1938 and not replaced, until finally in 2010 the museum commissioned world-renowned artist Kiki Smith and the highly respected architect Deborah Gans to create a new window. The goal was to make something that would blend with the motifs of the synagogue and respect its history yet be original in its design. At its center is a prominent Star of David from which a bronze pinwheel configuration emanates, all set against a field of traditional mouth-blown blue and silver stained glass, carpeted with five-pointed stars mimicking the dome and the celestially decorated walls.

This meticulously restored building now hosts a wide array of events and exhibits, such as literary series, photographic exhibits, and site-specific art installations. A member of the American Association of Museums, Eldridge also hosts a variety of multicultural festivals including the very popular annual Egg Rolls, Egg Creams, and Empanadas Street Festival.

Shrine Church of the Most Precious Blood

113 Baxter Street

The Home of the "Feast of Feasts"

ROMAN CATHOLIC
CORNERSTONE LAID 1901

The Italian immigrants who flooded the tenements of the Lower East Side were not welcomed into the community. The more established New Yorkers, albeit also tenement dwellers, forbade them to worship in their sanctuaries—however, they deigned to allow them to worship in their church basements. To address this problem, in 1888 the Vatican called for a national parish to serve the Italian population. After this, the Scalabrini Fathers purchased land at 113 Baxter Street and construction began on the Church of the Most Precious Blood, based on designs by Schickel & Ditmars architectural firm. While their earlier designs reflected German Gothic influences, Most Precious Blood displays a more Italian Franciscan style. The cornerstone for the new church was laid on July 7, 1901, which meant that the congregation could move out of the basement of the Church of the Transfiguration. By 1904, the infrastructure and basic interior elements were completed, and reflect Neapolitan Baroque style.

San Gennaro (St. Januarius), a fourth-century Roman martyr, is the patron saint of Naples. The celebration of San Gennaro was initiated in this church as a solemn mass. But in 1926, Most Precious Blood decided to have a one-day block party for their patron saint and took the statue of San Gennaro from the church, carrying it aloft along Baxter street. Over the years the procession and celebration grew, and now each September throngs pour into Little Italy for the Feast of San Gennaro, aka the "Feast of Feasts."

The church is named for the "Miracle of San Gennaro." Three times a year, a vial containing the martyr's dried blood is displayed in Naples Cathedral and the faithful pray for its liquefaction. Here in the U.S., Most Precious Blood is the national Shrine Church of San Gennaro and houses a vial of the dried seventeen-hundred-year-old blood.

St. Mary Grand

440 Grand Street

The Church of Ellis Island's First Immigrant

ROMAN CATHOLIC
CORNERSTONE LAID 1832

Founded in 1826 by Irish immigrants, St. Mary's is the third-oldest Roman Catholic church in New York, following St. Peter's on Barclay Street and the Basilica of Old St. Patrick's on Mulberry Street. It was a rocky beginning. At the time, the Know-Nothing party was composed of extremists known as nativists, who demonstrated vociferously and violently against immigrants and Catholics—multitudes of whom were both.

The parish's first home was on Sheriff Street in the former Seventh Presbyterian Church. It was here that, only five years after the church was established on Guy Fawkes night, November 5, 1831, a lone arsonist—a member of the Know-Nothing party—set the church ablaze. Father Luke Berry rushed to ring the bell to send an alert but it had been silenced with rags.

The bell held special significance. At the time, the penal code in Ireland forbade chapels from having bells and the custom carried over in the New World—briefly. St. Mary's was the first Catholic church in New York to have a bell.

In a stroke of divine irony, only the bell—and the church's safe—survived the conflagration. A month after Father Berry singlehandedly fought the blaze, exhausted and injured, he died and was buried in the cemetery at the Basilica of Old St. Patrick's.

A year after the fire, in 1832, the congregation purchased the land where the church currently stands, and a cornerstone was laid for a new church. It was designed in the style of Greek Revival that was the popular architecture of the time. Only seventeen months after groundbreaking, the church opened. Three decades or so later, the renowned ecclesiastical Irish architect Patrick C. Keely was hired for a major renovation during which the facade was stripped and replaced with one of Romanesque form. In 1840, a Georgian-style bell and clock tower were erected above the entrance.

While the Romanesque exterior of the building is very simplified and unadorned, the interior houses some spectacular highlights. A glass dome spills light into the sanctuary and a stained glass skylight bathes the chancel in softly hued light.

As immigrants continued to pour into the country, St. Mary's survived the horrific draft riots and the Civil War to welcome these "huddled masses . . . your tired, your poor." In 1904, one such immigrant entered the sanctuary—Annie Moore, who was the first immigrant to pass through the inspection station of Ellis Island. Moore became a member of the church and spearheaded a campaign to embellish the church with a new cupola.

Besides the throngs of Irish immigrants were waves of Jewish immigrants who peaceably shared the wretched spaces of Lower Manhattan's tenements, two of the many ingredients of New York's revered "melting pot." Certain incidents of coexisting would unsettle various constituencies. One such incident was when Simon Koppe, PhD, born of Orthodox Jewish parents (who may have exclaimed, "Oy Vey!"), became a member of St. Mary's. He was subsequently baptized into the Catholic faith, and received his first communion in St. Mary's on May 25, 1890. His eleven-month-old baby had previously been baptized.

Bialystoker Synagogue

7–11 Bialystoker Place

What's a Lobster Doing
in a Place Like This?

ORTHODOX JUDAISM
BUILT 1826

When a group of Jews from Bialystok, Poland, immigrated to New York in the 1820s, they brought a major—and minor—part of their heritage with them. The minor is a culinary treat called a bialy, which is the Polish city's take on a bagel that with a schmear or a dollop of butter is a comforting palate pleaser. But the more significant part of their traditions that traveled across the sea was the practice of their religion. The Bialystoker Synagogue was founded in 1865 on Manhattan's Lower East Side. The congregation known as Chevra Anshei Chesed of Bialystok first worshipped at locations on Hester Street and then on Orchard Street. By 1905, the wave of immigrants from Bialystok was such that the congregation merged with another from the same Polish region, Hadas Yeshuan, and the Bait Ha'Knesset Anshi Bialystoker, also known as the Bialystoker Synagogue, was born.

The congregation purchased the building from a Methodist church located at 7 Willet Street, where it still stands, although its current official address is 7–11 Bialystoker Place. The street name was changed to honor the synagogue. The Federal-style structure is made of hyperlocal Manhattan schist from a quarry on Pitt Street. It is one of only four early nineteenth-century fieldstone religious buildings that survive from the late Federal period in Lower Manhattan, according to the synagogue's website.

Characteristic of Methodist churches is an austere design as seen in the simple stone facade of the Bialystoker, which has few embellishments other than its three tall arched windows and imposing doors. Some of the original unembellished wooden pews are still used today. The original walls of the Methodist church, according to an article by Richard McBee, were likely to have echoed the austerity of the exterior with unassertive whitewashed walls. But not today.

46

A peek inside the ark, revealing some of the Torahs within

The facade belies the visual riot of grandeur that awaits inside and announces itself with an elaborately painted ceiling. A colossal ark that houses the Torah is bookmarked by two floor-to-ceiling stained glass windows. All is illuminated by natural light as well as three dazzling chandeliers that were added during a 1988 renovation. The resplendence is but one of many intriguing incongruities rife in this house of worship. Not only does the heavily embellished interior contradict the puritanical foundations of its original Protestant inhabitants, but it also was

    LOWER MANHATTAN

View of the enigmatic lobster, defying all kosher laws!

a product of the Great Depression, an era marked by endemic deprivation, not opulence. Instead of succumbing to despair, a decision was made around 1929 to beautify the space "to provide a sense of hope and inspiration to the community," as David Koegel writes on the Bialystoker's website.

Another incongruity is the curious depiction of a lobster among the equally incongruous panels that depict the signs of the zodiac, defying Hebrew scripture that states "no sign of the zodiac has power over Israel," not to mention the general prohibition of images of idolatry. The panels, set against a ceiling awash in a symphony of blue sky with airy clouds and framed by Corinthian columns, were likely painted by an artist familiar with rococo and baroque ornamentation, McBee speculates. He also offers a possible explanation for odd adornment by showing how the signs of the zodiac can reflect the Hebrew calendar. For instance, he posits, the springtime ram of Aries is transformed into the lamb of Mazel Nisan, the Hebrew month of Passover. Remaining a mystery is why Cancer, the crab, has been transformed into a lobster, in that all shellfish are forbidden in the Kosher dietary laws of Judaism.

As is typical in an Orthodox Jewish congregation like Bialystoker, the men and women are separated. A balcony section accommodates female congregants. In the corner of the balcony is a hidden door behind which a ladder is found that leads to an attic. Shortly after it opened, this secret attic was purportedly a stop on the Underground Railroad.

Kehila Kedosha Janina Synagogue and Museum

280 Broome Street

The Only Romaniote Synagogue in
the Western Hemisphere

ROMANIOTE JUDAISM
BUILT 1925–27

Legend has it that around AD 70, a group of Jewish prisoners were aboard a ship to Rome, bound for slavery, when a storm struck, tossing the ship ashore in Greece. The Jews made their way to the small city of Ioannina. For two thousand years it has remained home to a community of Jews that are neither Sephardic nor Ashkenazi, but Romaniote Jews who are considered Greek Jews. While adopting Greek customs, they fiercely held on to their Jewish traditions that have now survived two millennia.

In the early twentieth century, these Romaniote Jews were among the hordes of immigrants greeted by Lady Liberty. Upon arrival, while there were already by this time hundreds of synagogues for the Yiddish-speaking Ashkenazi and the Spanish-speaking Sephardic Jews, they found no place to practice their special brand of the faith. So, in 1906, the Romaniotes organized their own congregation. From 1925 to 1927 they built a synagogue at 280 Broome Street that remains the only Romaniote synagogue in the western hemisphere.

To ensure the preservation of its heritage, the synagogue is also home to a vibrant museum built into the second-floor women's gallery. Thus Kehila Kedosha Janina serves as the mother synagogue for Romaniotes around the world. Most of the hundreds of other synagogues that were part of the busy hustle-bustle that was the Lower East Side at the turn of the century no longer exist; while other synagogue buildings remain extant, they are no longer houses of worship for Jews. Kehila Kedosha Janina survived and remains a thriving part of the neighborhood.

The brick and stone building was designed by Sidney Daub with a blend of classical and Moorish architectural traditions and details. The main entrance has a cusped (intersections of scalloped forms) architecture while the second-story windows are topped by semicircular keyed arches. Copper Stars of David adorn the

50

peak and parapet; tablets of Jewish law are set within a stone arch slightly above and centered between the second-story windows. Inside, modest elements such as the pressed tin ceiling are set against more ornate decor. Some of the stained glass windows house Stars of David made of golden-hued glass. Others combine floral motifs with other Jewish symbols.

First Roumanian American Congregation

89–93 Rivington Street

"The Cantor's Carnegie Hall"

ORTHODOX JUDAISM
BUILT 1888 (DEMOLISHED 2006)

When it was built in 1888, the redbrick Romanesque Revival building was home to the Allen Street Methodist Episcopal Church and subsequently several other religious groups, both Jewish and Christian. The First Roumanian American Congregation, known as the Congregation Shaarey Shamoyim (Gates of Heaven) and dating back to 1860, bought the building in 1902, and for more than one hundred years it thrived, often filling its 1,700 seats.

In its heyday it was known as the "Cantor's Carnegie Hall," having attracted the most talented cantors, including Moishe Oysher, who was known as one of the greatest cantorial singers. The choir could boast some boldface names as well, including Red Buttons and Eddie Cantor. Among its members was another famous comedian: George Burns.

In the latter half of the twentieth century, as its membership and, consequentially, funding declined, the building fell into disrepair. After the roof collapsed, the building was deemed unstable and would require major renovations that the congregation could not afford. It was demolished in 2006.

Basilica of St. Patrick's Old Cathedral

263 Mulberry Street

"Old St. Pat's"

Roman Catholic
Cornerstone Laid 1809

To many, the grand neo-Gothic St. Patrick's Cathedral in Midtown Manhattan on posh Fifth Avenue symbolizes the Roman Catholic Church in America—and it certainly is a top-of-the-list tourist attraction. But this celebrated cathedral is but a younger and, frankly, less storied version of the original St. Patrick's Cathedral in New York. The original, now officially named the Basilica of St. Patrick's Old Cathedral but fondly known as "Old St. Pat's," is found at 263 Mulberry in Little Italy and has been the crossroads of immigrant groups for centuries: the Irish preceded the Italians, the Dominicans succeeded the Italians, and more recently, a significant Chinese population has found a home here, where mass is often offered in various languages to suit the congregants.

Old St. Pat's is quintessential New York. Its cup runneth over with New York history, celebrity connections, and personal narratives of the city's richest and poorest. Now a parish church, it began its life as the seat of the Diocese, and later Archdiocese, of New York. It was the city's first cathedral and second church. It is here that the first cardinal of the New World, John McCloskey, received his red hat.

While it was being built from 1809 to 1815, the Irish were the dominant Catholic group, and thus it was named for the patron saint of Ireland, St. Patrick, and was the first church in America to honor this saint. Many symbols of the subsequent waves of immigrants through the centuries are evident throughout the church—the stained glass windows have depictions of San Gennaro, the patron saint of Naples, while a special chapel is dedicated to Our Lady of Altagracia, the patroness and Blessed Mother of the Dominican Republic.

The roots of the old cathedral are found in a graveyard of the first Catholic church in New York, St. Peter's (see page 28). St. Peter's was built at a time when it was

56

traditional to be buried on the grounds of one's house of worship. (A graveyard, as opposed to a cemetery, refers to the burial ground attached to a church. A cemetery has no association with a church.) Within a few decades, with more and more Catholics living—and thus dying—in Manhattan, every inch of the graveyard was packed with tombstones and what lay beneath, necessitating the parish to purchase land to use as a cemetery. They bought land farther north on what was the Tupper Farm, in an area that was still rural land but eventually became the site where Old St. Pat's was erected.

By 1808, in response to a growing number of Catholic immigrants, Pope Pius VII established the Diocese of New York, which included all New York State and a portion of northern New Jersey. More room was needed not just for the dead, but for the living as well. Small donations came from multitudes of poor Irish immigrants, with larger donations coming from wealthy Irish Catholic immigrants, including Cornelius Heeney, a business partner of John Jacob Astor (yes, *those* Astors). On June 8, 1809, the cornerstone was laid for the city's first cathedral, second Catholic church, and the second Roman Catholic cathedral in America. (Baltimore's cathedral was the first.)

Throughout its more than two-hundred-year-old history, Old St. Pat's has had a long list of famous names—of both the religious and Hollywood-style variety— as well as many star-studded events. The basilica was the set for one of the most familiar and powerful scenes in cinematic history—the baptism of the nephew of Michael Corleone (played by Al Pacino) in Francis Ford Coppola's *The Godfather*. While Michael is renouncing Satan in order to become the godfather to his sister's baby, his hitmen are in various dark corners of the country slaughtering his enemies.

The church is near and dear to a former altar boy and now famous director and film impresario: Martin Scorsese, who grew up only a block away. It was his childhood parish, and he claims his youthful imagination was fueled by the basilica. It is featured in two of his major films: *Gangs of New York* and *Mean Streets*. In the former, employing a large dose of artistic license, he recreates the very real plots (one in 1836, one in 1844) by anti-Catholic nativists—and their organized gangs such as the Know-Nothings—to sack the church. In *Mean Streets*, Charlie (played by Harvey Keitel) and Johnny Boy (played by Robert De Niro) have a heart-to-heart within the safe enclosure of the churchyard.

The wall that protects Charlie and Johnny Boy was built in 1836 and still stands today. In the real world of 1836, word got out about the gangs' plans to attack, prompting parishioners and others from the neighborhood to quickly build the fortifying wall. It proved its lasting usefulness during the civil unrest in the summer of 2020 when, in the wake of the George Floyd murder, it became a canvas for graffiti (albeit not anti-Catholic) and kept the damage to a minimum—a single church window was broken.

Today, Scorsese is helping spearhead the mission to restore and preserve the church's 1868 organ built by New Yorker Henry Erben, who was considered the leading American organ builder at the time. An artistic and technological masterpiece, the organ is the only one of its kind in its original acoustic space. Built after the 1866 fire, with numerous small donations from the parishioners and others from the neighborhood, it sent a message to New York that the immigrants were here to stay.

Nearly two hundred years ago, in 1826, a unique encounter occurred between three remarkable people: Mozart's librettist, Lorenzo Da Ponte, who was saddled with debt and selling groceries; opera's first diva, Maria Malibran, all of seventeen years old; and Pierre Toussaint, a former slave and benefactor of the church. The Sisters of Charity were building an orphanage and needed money, so with the help of Toussaint and Da Ponte, a fundraising event was planned—the headliner was Malibran. Comparable to today's star-studded Met Gala, the oratorio attracted a who's who of New York and raised the needed funds. Just as significant, it was a spiritual and musical concert that introduced opera to New Yorkers.

The Oratorio, a recreation of that event, took place in October 2018. In attendance were members of today's Sisters of Charity, who were overcome by emotion with the realization that they were listening to the same music in the same space with the same organ as their sisters had two centuries earlier. One element that could not be recreated was Malibran's preternatural talent—it took two women to reach the same range she did solo.

Pierre Toussaint, although a member of St. Peter's Church, was also associated with Old St. Pat's and was one of its most magnanimous benefactors. He was buried in the graveyard of Old St. Pat's in 1853 and his headstone still marks the site, but his remains have since been moved to St. Patrick's Cathedral on Fifth Avenue.

Among other tombstones of notable citizens is that of Elizabeth Ann Seton. She opened the first Catholic girls' school in Baltimore in 1808, founded the Sisters of Charity that established orphanages and hospitals throughout the country, and helped develop the parochial school system in America. Mother Elizabeth Ann Seton was canonized by Pope Paul VI in 1975.

The original St. Patrick's was designed by Joseph-François Mangin, who also was a codesigner of City Hall. One of the earliest Gothic Revival structures in the country, it was also the largest church in the city at 120 feet long and 80 feet wide. After the cathedral's destruction by fire in 1866, it was rebuilt with designs by Henry Engelbert. The church and its other campus buildings were among the first sites to be designated as New York City landmarks in 1966, and in 1977 it was granted a spot on the National Register of Historic Places.

In Memory of
the Deceased Members of the
Cude and ... Families

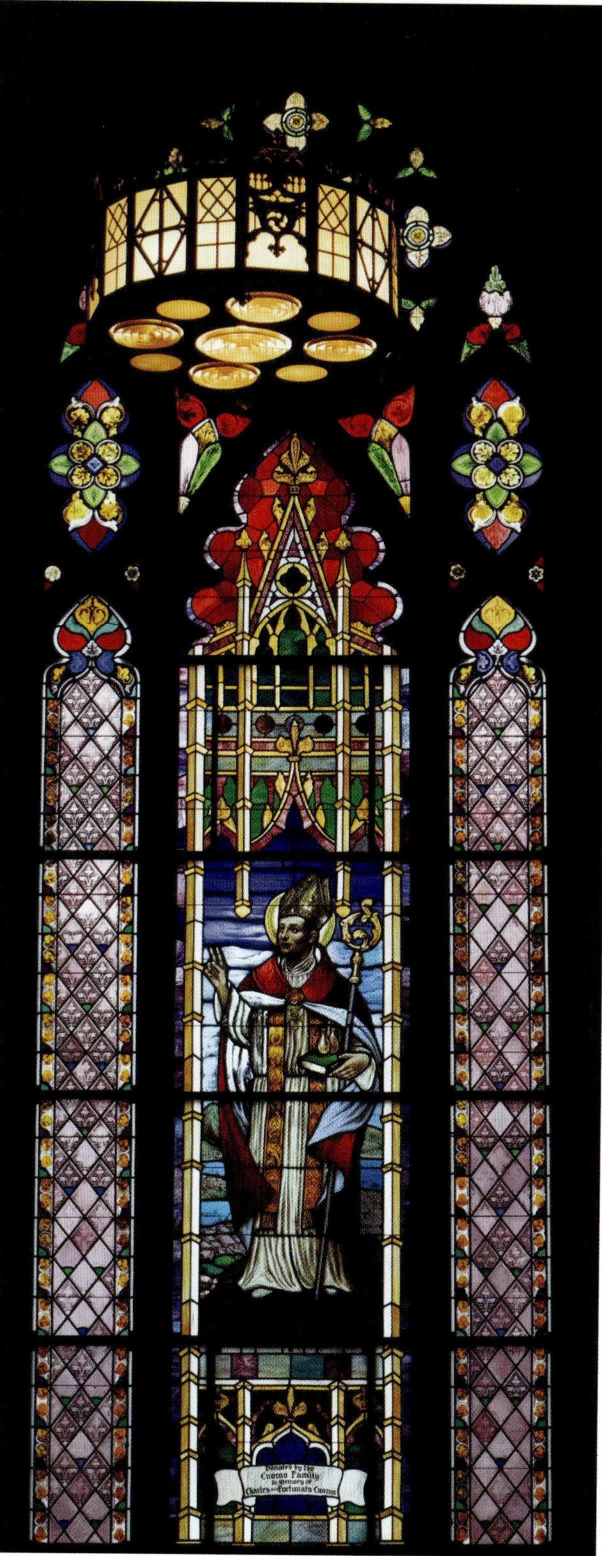

Donated by the
Cuomo Family
In memory of
Charles and Fortunate Cuomo

Soho, Greenwich Village, and Chelsea

St. Joseph's Church

371 Sixth Avenue

"The Grandeur of the Divine Service"

ROMAN CATHOLIC
CORNERSTONE LAID 1833

St. Joseph's Church was the sixth Catholic parish church and the second largest (after "Old" St. Patrick's) in New York when it was erected in 1833. Founded four years earlier by Bishop John Dubois, the first pastor, Reverend Patrick Duffy, initially conducted services in a rented hall near Christopher Street.

The dedication of the church, on Sunday, March 16, was attended by a veritable who's who in the Catholic Archdiocese of New York, as well as key figures in the early history of New York. Among them were Bishop Dubois; Father John Hughes, who later became archbishop of New York; and Father John McCloskey, who became pastor of St. Joseph's and eventually the first US cardinal. The press took notice. One newspaper wrote, "Never before have we witnessed anything more impressive, more solemn, or more august than the grandeur of the Divine Service."

The original Greek Revival structure, designed by John Doran, still stands, but the interior suffered damage during two fires, in 1855 and 1885. The stained glass windows, dating from 1879, survived and are intact today, but after 1885, renovations to the interior were made. In 1972, Father Robert Wilde, pastor at the time, tore out the sanctuary, including the high altar and all the marble work, replacing it with what the church's website describes as "a bare sanctuary that parishioners of [the] time complained was Protestant in appearance."

The denuding wasn't entirely a fiasco when the Transfiguration fresco, created in 1835, was revealed under layers of paint and restored. It was modeled after a work of Raphael's that is in the Vatican.

Major renovation and restoration work was also done from 2019 to 2020 on both the exterior and interior. Statues that had been removed by Father Wilde were repaired and returned to the sanctuary, and an impressive organ was built by Orgues Létourneau Ltée.

ABOVE
The Transfiguration
fresco (center) was
uncovered during
church renovations.

RIGHT
An impressive window
meets an arched railing
and humble staircase.

OPPOSITE ABOVE
The monumental organ
at the rear of the church

OPPOSITE BELOW
The trumpets and
flutes of the organ

St. Nicholas of Myra Orthodox Church

288 East 10th Street

A Restrained Gothic from Renwick

CARPATHO-RUSSIAN ORTHODOX
BUILT 1882–83

The elegantly simple Renaissance Revival church at 288 East 10th Street, designed by renowned architect James Renwick, has been home to St. Nicholas of Myra Orthodox Church, a parish of the American Carpatho-Russian Orthodox Diocese of the USA, since 1925. It was founded by immigrants of the Carpatho-Rusyn regions of present-day Slovakia, Poland, and Western Ukraine.

St. Nicholas of Myra's history began prior to the formation of the diocese when John Vislocky, who became reverend father deacon of St. Nicholas of Myra, approached Bishop Dzubaj (known as an exarch in the Orthodox church) about the possibility of founding a parish. In the home of a delicatessen owner, John Vanicky, plans were drawn up to form a new Orthodox church whose parishioners mostly came from the villages of Jarabina and Litmanová in the Tatra mountains, the highest range of the Central Carpathians that line the Polish–Slovakian border.

It wasn't until later that the diocese was formed, when American Carpatho-Russian Orthodox followers were concerned about the latinization attempts by the Roman Catholic Church. They organized a church congress to steer the future of their faith. The diocese was established in 1938 and is under the canonical protection of Ecumenical Patriarchate of Constantinople.

The first services of St. Nicholas of Myra—named for the archbishop of Myra (located in modern-day Turkey) who is a patron saint of children, sailors, merchants, and students—were held in September 1925. That same fall, the congregation rented space from the Episcopal Diocese of New York at its current location at 288 East 10th Street for $50 a month in what was the Holy Trinity Slovak Lutheran Church. St. Nicholas wasn't able to rent the entire building at that time—part of it was the Leonardo Da Vinci School of Art, but later, with a doubled rent of $100 a month, the entire building was theirs to occupy.

68

The structure was originally designed and built from 1882 to 1883 as the Memorial Chapel of St. Mark's Church-in-the-Bowery. The Episcopal memorial chapel was funded by the Rutherford-Stuyvesant family, descendants of Peter Stuyvesant, director general (essentially governor) of the colony of New Netherland in the mid-seventeenth century. When the English showed up to conquer the colony, his despotic nature meant that he had few allies willing to support him and he was forced to surrender. He went back to Holland but eventually returned and settled on his farm in the "Bouwerie," where he died in 1672. His body is entombed in the church.

The simplified Gothic style executed with Renaissance Revival influences is certainly not as grand as any of Renwick's earlier projects, notably St. Patrick's Cathedral and Grace Church. He may have taken on this more modest commission because his son Henry B. Renwick was on the board—along with other prominent New Yorkers, including Hamilton Fish, a former governor of New York State and secretary of state under President Grant. "Its style was considered appropriate for its purpose and use as a place of worship and education for the poor immigrant population of the Lower East Side at that time," reads the church's website. Nevertheless, the church does display terra-cotta ornaments, hooded lancet windows

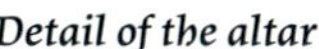

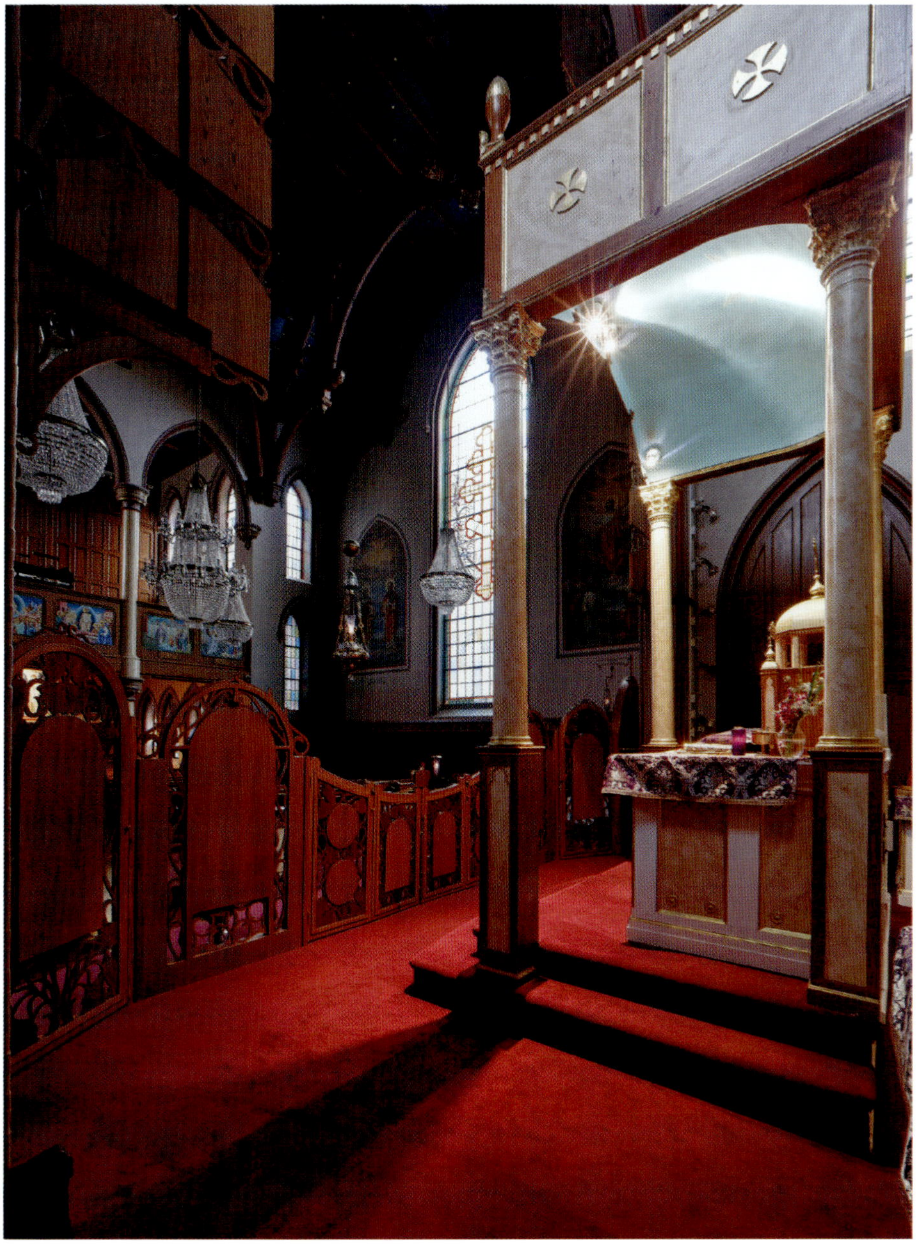

Detail of the altar

(a narrow, tall window topped with an acute pointed arch) with stained glass, and decorative moldings on the doorways.

Crowning the section on the corner of 10th Street and Avenue A, which is home to the library and school of the parish, is a tall, square bell tower with a steep pyramidal roof. On the front is a terra-cotta bas-relief of a lion, which is a symbol of St. Mark the Evangelist and had sacred meaning for the original Episcopalian congregation. The gable end faces the street and is distinguished by three tall, Gothic arched windows united by a pointed-arch lintel. Orthodox-style copper crosses crown the chapel, entrance porch, and the tower.

First Presbyterian Church

12 West 12th Street

"Old First"

Harking back almost as far as Trinity Church, the oldest parish in New York City, the First Presbyterian Church celebrated its tricentennial in 2016. The roots of the congregation go back even further to the first decade of the 1700s when Francis Makemie, a Scots-Irish clergyman, played an important role in establishing the Presbyterian Church in the colonies. It wasn't easy. Only Anglicans following the Church of England were legally licensed to preach and worship in the city, so Makemie broke the law. He preached publicly to a small group in a private home, was arrested, and then subsequently acquitted, an event that became a catalyst for about eighty New Yorkers to organize themselves and found the Church of Scotland.

Their first home was a modest building on Wall Street—not far from Trinity—where their brand of Christianity was decidedly not welcome. The first service was held in 1719 and after some internal divisions between the progressives and the conservatives, it experienced rapid growth during the evangelical movement of the 1730s and 1740s. To accommodate the growing numbers, the church was expanded and a steeple and bell were added. By 1768, the congregation had grown to three hundred and the walls of the original church were bursting. This time, instead of enlarging the church, they built a second structure, known as the "Brick Church," at the corner of Nassau and Beekman Streets. Services were held in both locations.

With the Revolutionary War approaching, fissures between the Anglicans (Episcopalians) and the Presbyterians widened. As an arm of the Church of England, the Episcopalians supported the king and parliament. Presbyterians, on the other hand, were zealous patriots and many served in the Continental Army, thus the war was sometimes called the "Presbyterian rebellion." The British used the church on Wall Street as a barracks and stable, thus forcing the closure of it as well as the newer Brick Church.

Following the war, the relationship between the Presbyterians and Episcopalians improved. The Presbyterian chapels were damaged during the war, and in the aftermath the Episcopalians lent their parish's chapels for worship. Around the time the Brick Church reopened in 1784, with the Wall Street building reopening soon after, the Presbyterian Church became the first religious organization to receive a charter from the state of New York. Its official name became the First Presbyterian Church in the City of New York, known familiarly as simply "First Church" and then, as the years passed, "Old First."

By 1811, the building was indeed old and was completely rebuilt, only to be destroyed by a devastating fire that decimated much of Lower Manhattan in 1835. By this time, the population was migrating uptown, so the church followed its flock and acquired the property on Fifth Avenue in the heart of Greenwich Village, where it remains very much alive today. The architect Joseph C. Wells designed the soaring Gothic structure, modeled after St. Saviour's Church in Bath, England, while the tower was inspired by the one atop Magdalen College in Oxford. The new church was dedicated in 1846 when the congregation began to worship there.

The south transept was designed by McKim, Mead & White but wasn't added to the building until 1893. Two years later, First Presbyterian merged with its close-by congregations, Madison Square Church and University Place Church. The Greenwich Village church became home to all three but the pulpit hails from University Place and the baptismal font from Madison Square.

Then in the 1920s, a brouhaha erupted with the preaching of the Reverend Harry Emerson Fosdick. He proclaimed that Darwinism was not at odds with the Christian faith. To say that his pronouncements did not go over well with the First Church congregants and the larger Christian community is a gross understatement. A roiling national controversy ensued. Fosdick, three years after his Darwin declaration, resigned, only to be approached in 1925 by John D. Rockefeller. He asked Fosdick to head the Park Avenue Baptist Church, which was soon to move to the Rockefeller-built Riverside Church on the West Side. Fosdick declined on the grounds that he did not want to be known "as the pastor of the richest man in the country." Rockefeller immediately retorted, "Do you think that more people will criticize you on account of my wealth than will criticize me on account of your theology?" Fosdick eventually accepted, on the condition that the church be nondenominational, and he remained pastor at Riverside Church until 1946.

Grace Church

802 Broadway

"A Bastion of High Society"

EPISCOPAL
BUILT 1843–46

It's not what you know—it's who you know. That somewhat cynical adage forms the foundation of Grace Church, which stands today at 802 Broadway, as well as the career of the world-renowned architect James Renwick, who is considered one of the most important architects of the nineteenth century. Grace Church was his maiden project.

Around 1806, Grace Church's history began in a humbler manner, in a modest building at the corner of Broadway and Rector Street, approximately two miles south of where it stands today. By 1834, with the pulse—and population—of the city moving northward, its fourth rector, Thomas House Taylor, became concerned that the church would languish in its current location. He convinced the congregation that an uptown move was essential for the church to flourish.

Nine years later in 1843, the church purchased property that was then an apple orchard owned by Henry Brevoort Jr., located at Broadway between 10th and 11th Streets. Brevoort was landed gentry—descended from Dutch stock—who inherited a vast estate in Manhattan. He was a friend of the literary lion of the times, Washington Irving, with whom he traveled throughout Europe.

The setting for the church is a point where Broadway bends toward the west. Its site allowed it to be seen from the original church's location, and today its unusual positioning makes it viewable from as far away as City Hall. According to David W. Dunlap, the bend was due to Henry Brevoort resisting efforts to straighten the road through his apple orchard.

Land in hand, the search for an architect began. Multiple designs and bids were submitted from highly established architects throughout the city. None of them were selected. Instead, the commission went to a civil engineer whose only major work to date had been designing part of the Croton Reservoir at 42nd Street. What

76

James Renwick Jr. lacked in terms of real architectural bona fides was compensated in spades by his family's social standing, influence, and connections. His father, James Renwick Sr., was part of the faculty of Columbia College. A gifted student, Renwick Jr. began attending classes there at age twelve, earning an undergraduate degree and a masters by 1836.

However proficient he may have been as an engineer, such skills would certainly not place him at the top of the bidding list. But he had a major advantage—Henry Brevoort was his maternal uncle—and he had family members in the church's vestry. An act of shameless nepotism indeed, but one that launched the architectural career of Renwick.

Prior to breaking ground, the rector, Thomas House Taylor, embarked on a tour of Europe to study the design of churches throughout the continent. Upon his return he was "adamant" that the new church be in the Gothic style. Renwick was eager to oblige and engaged in intensive study of Gothic design. The building was consecrated on March 7, 1846, and still stands today. Avoiding the fate of so many of New York's nineteenth-century churches, Grace Church did not endure dilapidation and abandonment, but rather its grandeur has advanced over time.

Not everyone agreed that the church was an architectural triumph. In an article in the September 1853 issue of *Putnam's Monthly Magazine of American Literature, Science and Art*, an unnamed author submitted a scathing review of the city's ecclesiastical architecture in general, and Grace Church specifically. "There are two causes for the incorrect and unimposing architecture of the greater number of churches in New York; the one is the incapacity of the architects who design them—the other is the ignorance of the people who pay for them. . . . Grace Church is no credit to the architect who built it. . . . The interior is like a poor kaleidoscope."

Fortunately, it was other opinions that prevailed. Mr. Dale Owen's *Hints on the Architecture of Public Buildings*, as quoted in the *Putnam's* article, called it "a sparkling specimen, on a small scale, of a cathedral with transept in the style of Gothic prevailing on the European continent about the commencement of the fifteenth century."

Its sparkle has only become brighter. The original windows of lightly tinted glass were replaced in the late nineteenth century with vividly colored stained glass windows, designed by Clayton & Bell and Henry Holiday, that tell Old Testament stories. The steeple, originally made of wood, was replaced in 1883 with the august marble spire that rises today.

The original wooden steeple was a source of scandal and rumor, not only to *Putnam's* critic, who found any poor imitations of fifteenth-century Gothic style unacceptable, but to the congregation, who for a time believed that Renwick failed to make the building strong enough to bear the weight of a stone spire. However, it is said that the rumor was put to rest when the Episcopal clergy admitted—from the pulpit—that it was lack of money, not structural strength, that necessitated the wooden spire.

In its heyday, Grace Church "was a bastion of high society. 'To be married or buried within its walls has been ever considered the height of felicity,'" says Dunlap, quoting an unknown source.

Grace Church

Church of St. Francis Xavier

46 West 16th Street

Home of the "Waterfront Priest"

ROMAN CATHOLIC
CORNERSTONE LAID 1878

In a kind of six-degrees-of-separation way, the Church of St. Francis Xavier is part of *On the Waterfront*, Elia Kazan's 1954 film that won eight Academy Awards, including Best Picture, Best Director for Kazan, and Best Actor and Best Supporting Actress for Marlon Brando and Eva Marie Saint respectively. Karl Malden was nominated for Best Supporting Actor for his portrayal of Father Barry, who ministers to the tough longshoremen subjected to abuse through union and mob corruption. Father Barry's character was based on St. Francis Xavier's true-life Jesuit priest, the Reverend John M. Corridan. Like his fictional incarnation, Reverend Corridan worked on the docks—his *New York Times* 1984 obituary said that he "made the harbor his parish" and became known as the "Waterfront Priest." He helped with the formation of the Waterfront Commission of New York Harbor in 1953 with both New York and New Jersey legislatures.

Budd Schulberg, who wrote the screenplay for *On The Waterfront*, had gone to Father Corridan for advice on the script. "I found," he wrote, "a tall, gangling, balding, energetic, ruddy-faced Irishman whose speech was a fascinating blend of Hell's Kitchen jargon, baseball slang, the facts and figures of a master in economics, and the undeniable humanity of Christ."

The roots of St. Francis Xavier were planted about a century before Father Corridan was ordained. In 1847, John Larkin, a Jesuit priest, was tasked with founding a church in Manhattan—with a treasure amounting to all of fifty cents. A mass was offered to raise more realistic funds, and in the pews was a French muralist who had recently arrived on New York's shores and was giving thanks to God for his family's safe journey. Wary of the banks in his new homeland, he asked Father Larkin for advice on what to do with his $5,000 to keep it safe.

Meanwhile, a Protestant church between Bowery and Elizabeth "had just suffered

a great schism," the website of St. Francis Xavier says, and the building became available for purchase at a price of $18,000 with a down payment of $5,000 necessary to seal the deal. "Recognizing God's intervention when he saw it," according to the website, Father Larkin offered the faithful Frenchman security for his money in return for the mortgage payment.

Unfortunately, that property burned shortly after the Jesuit community had moved in. Yet in spite of his superiors urging him to give up altogether, Larkin and his parishioners vowed to renew, renovate, and rebuild the church. They succeeded handily, and in March 1851 a new church was dedicated on West 16th Street, along with the College of St. Francis Xavier on West 15th Street.

Two and a half decades later, tragedy struck. Someone needlessly shouted, "Fire!" during a service when there was no fire, but in the panicked evacuation, seven people died. In the aftermath of this catastrophe, the Jesuits decided to build a new church, which still stands today. It was designed by the prolific and well-known Irish ecclesiastical architect Patrick C. Keely, who hailed from Brooklyn. The cornerstone was laid on May 5, 1878, with five thousand people in attendance.

Keely was known for his Gothic designs, but for St. Francis Xavier he created a vibrant building in the style of a classical Roman basilica. The granite walls of the interior of the church feature frescoed medallions on the barrel-vaulted ceiling that rises about seventy-four feet high. There are five altars all built of marble with pillars of Mexican and Californian onyx.

Among the highlights of the magnificent interior is the baptismal font and pool that were integrated into the reredos during renovation and restoration undertaken from 2000 to 2010. The pool floor is adorned with intricate mosaic that imitates the design of the stained glass windows. The Blessed Virgin Mary altar is embellished by a Tiffany-designed stained glass window of the Madonna and Child with St. Francis of Assisi and St. Claire. Another stained glass window designed by Tiffany adorns the St. Joseph altar. Both windows bear the Tiffany signature.

On the main level, the artist William Lamprecht, a German immigrant, painted murals depicting the fourteen stations of the cross that were restored during the renovation. The artist's intent was for the vibrant colors to gradually darken as one follows the story of Jesus's last hours. The mezzanine level is ornamented with thirty statues of the saints.

In recognition of current issues worthy of prayer and reflection, one of the altars is the HIV/AIDS Altar of Remembrance, which is dedicated to all those living with the disease and those who died from it. Inscriptions are welcome in the book of prayer.

St. George's Church

209 East 16th Street

Sanctity and Scandal

In 1749, when St. George's was founded as a chapel of Trinity Church, the vast majority of Manhattan's population was Episcopalian, and many had already attained significant wealth in the New World. St. George's was originally built at the corner of Beekman and Cliff Streets, a posh neighborhood at the time that attracted the beau monde. The original church that stood on the corner was built of impressive stone and held the first commencement of King's College, now Columbia University. St. George's became independent of Trinity in 1811. Three years later fire destroyed it, and it was rebuilt the following year, this time with an emblem of wealth: a steeple clock made by master clockmaker Simeon Willard of Roxbury, Massachusetts. For a time, St. George's clock was one of the most celebrated in the city.

By the mid-1800s, the bon ton was moving northward, and St. George's followed. In 1845, it laid the cornerstone for a new church on land donated by Peter G. Stuyvesant, now Stuyvesant Square. The old church was converted ignominiously to a stable, but Willard's famous clock was salvaged and was built into the steeple of the new church. Services began in the new structure in 1848, while construction was still ongoing. The Romanesque revival structure was not completed until 1856. Nine years later another fire erupted, destroying the interior and leaving only a shell. The well-funded congregation enabled rebuilding in just two years. Unfortunately, by 1888, the spires were deemed unsafe and taken down.

Among the well-heeled members of the congregation was J. P. Morgan, lending the church the moniker of "Mr. Morgan's Church." Among the other millionaires occupying the pews was Robert Fulton Cutting. The wedding of his daughter took place in the church in 1905 and was a social event that could compete with today's Met Gala. Among the A-list attendees was Miss Alice Roosevelt, the eldest

daughter of Theodore Roosevelt and a socialite extraordinaire. The funeral of J. P. Morgan in 1913 was also well-attended with fifteen hundred people within the walls of the church and throngs outside.

On April 18, 1920, after the sermon was completed, the vestrymen made their way down the aisles with the silver collection plates. In the pews were Herbert Satterlee, the son-in-law of J. P. Morgan, and Dr. James Wright Markoe, who had been Morgan's physician. When the plate reached Markoe's pew, a man who reached into his pocket, presumably to fill the silver plate, instead pulled out a revolver and shot the doctor in the head. While the killer tried to flee, Satterlee blocked his way using the collection plate, from which the gold and silver crashed noisily to the floor, and was fired at. The murderer, Thomas W. Simpkin, almost escaped but congregants overpowered and disarmed him. Apparently Simpkin had intended to kill J. P. Morgan himself, but when he learned that Morgan had been dead for seven years, he chose Markoe instead. He was convicted and committed to the Matteawan State Hospital for the Criminally Insane in Matteawan, New York, up the Hudson in what is now Dutchess County.

On a brighter note, the great composer and baritone Henry Thacker Burleigh, the grandson of former slaves, was a soloist in the choir at St. George's for fifty years. He had won the endorsement of J. P. Morgan at a time when many other churches didn't allow Blacks to worship in their churches. He was also a soloist at Temple Emanu-El for twenty-five years. Burleigh composed over two hundred works and was acclaimed for his own music as well as adaptations of African American spirituals. To please his maternal grandmother, he learned the music of Antonín Dvořák, who encouraged the young composer to preserve these melodies in his own compositions. In turn, Dvořák wrote themes inspired by the songs introduced to him by Burleigh in his Symphony No. 9 in E Minor (*From the New World*).

St. Peter's Episcopal Church

346 West 20th Street

"The Christmas Church"

EPISCOPAL
CORNERSTONE LAID 1836

St. Peter's Episcopal Church in Manhattan's Chelsea neighborhood is lovingly known as "The Christmas Church." While any and all Christian houses of worship could legitimately be called Christmas Churches in honor of the birthday of the man who made it all possible, St. Peter's has a different, but equally legitimate, claim to its moniker. The land upon which it sits was donated by Clement Clarke Moore, the author of one of the world's most beloved and familiar Christmas stories: "'Twas the Night Before Christmas."

The playful and witty poem that made Moore a household name was written solely to amuse his children. According to Rufus Rockwell Wilson's 1902 history, *New York Old & New: Its Story, Streets, and Landmarks*, light verse was not Moore's primary métier. He was a scholar, a teacher, and like his father before him, Bishop Benjamin Moore, Clement was fitted for the ministry, but never took orders. Instead, a bookworm who graduated from Columbia in 1798, he devoted himself to Oriental and Classical studies. "It was his custom to employ his leisure in writing verse," wrote Wilson, "not for profit or publication, but to lighten his severer labors." Among those labors was the first Hebrew-English lexicon. It was a houseguest who copied the poem and sent it to the *Sentinel*, a newspaper in upstate Troy, New York, that published it the following year during the holidays.

Yet according to both words and deeds, Moore himself possessed some Santa-like qualities. "Like his father before him, Clement C. Moore was, according to all testimony, a man of beautifully rounded character," Wilson said. Having descended from old New York aristocracy (i.e., "old money"), Moore had the means to allow his generous nature to do good deeds in concrete ways.

His good fortune was enabled by his father's mother-in-law, Molly Clarke, widow of Captain Thomas Clarke, a veteran of the French and Indian War. A few years

prior to his death in the middle of the eighteenth century, Captain Clarke made a daring real estate decision—he moved about three miles north of Greenwich Village to a stretch of rural land not far from the eastern shore of the Hudson River. He named the country estate he built Chelsea after a well-known hospital near London. While the area transformed from farmland to estate grounds to the home for the Episcopal seminary and finally to the very hip urban neighborhood it is now, the name, Chelsea, has endured for more than 250 years.

Unfortunately, not long after he settled into his new home Captain Clarke became ill. During this period of his infirmity, the estate went up in flames and he was rescued by neighbors and carried to a nearby farmhouse, where he soon died.

After a rather shockingly brief mourning period, his widow, Molly Clarke, rallied robustly and rebuilt an expanded estate. The new two-storied house sat approximately 200 feet west of today's Ninth Avenue with one of its corners on the

southern side of 23rd Street. Upon her death in 1802, the house and land—extending from Eighth Avenue and 19th Street to 24th Street and the Hudson—were bequeathed to her son-in-law, Bishop Benjamin Moore, and a little over a decade later to Clement Clarke Moore, his only son.

By the time Clement Moore inherited the property in 1813, the estate had for years been the seat of the General Theological Seminary of the Episcopal Church where he was one of its professors. Within a few years, Moore began opening the ninety-four acres to the existing streets and avenues of the city plan with the intent of fostering growth of the village. Part of this endeavor was giving a large swath of land rent-free to the seminary. Upon his death, he deeded the land to them.

The first part of St. Peter's to be built from 1831 to 1832 at 346 West 20th is now the rectory. When Moore donated the land, he envisioned a Greek Revival complex that would recall the Theseion (aka Temple of Hephaestus) in Athens. But it wasn't to be. Ecclesiastical architectural taste had abruptly shifted to Gothic Revival and that preference is on display in the tower and sanctuary that were designed by James W. Smith, erected in 1836, and still stand today at 344 West 20th.

The church was built from schist rock unearthed from the ground beneath it—giving St. Peter's a second moniker, "The Rock of Chelsea." But it wasn't until the 1950s that Moore was honored with his own piece of the rock when a tablet celebrating his magnanimity was affixed to the outer north wall of the old stone edifice.

An original door with detailed carvings in the Gothic style

An elegant, curving staircase receives the same level of care in its design as the rest of the church.

Midtown West

St. John the Baptist

213 West 30th Street

A Church with Nine Lives

ROMAN CATHOLIC
CORNERSTONE LAID 1871

Organized in 1840, St. John the Baptist was the second parish established to minister to German Catholics. (The first was St. Nicholas Church on the Lower East Side, established in 1833.) The newly formed congregation built a simple wooden structure, known as the German Roman Catholic Church of St. John, at 125 West 31st Street, but it had a short life—it was destroyed by fire in 1847. A new brick church was built nearby at 125 West 30th Street, and this one, too, was short-lived.

This time, it was internal problems that caused its demise. During this period, according to Barbara Brandes on the church's website, "the nascent Catholic Church in America suffered from Trusteeism, a practice which gave lay leaders of the church full and exclusive control of all parish affairs." Apparently the lay trustees of this church were so difficult to work with that no pastor lasted for more than a brief spell. In 1870, Archbishop Cardinal McCloskey was fed up and closed the church and asked the Order of Capuchin to take over. Fortunately the first Capuchin pastor, Father Bonaventure Frey, was able to bring harmony to the congregation. He tasked his parishioners to "express their devotion and ethnic pride" by building a more substantial and impressive edifice.

The acclaimed architect Napoleon LeBrun, who David W. Dunlap calls "a master of ecclesiastical architecture," was chosen for the new edifice and the cornerstone was laid in 1871. LeBrun's other works include the Cathedral Basilica of Saints Peter and Paul in Philadelphia, the Episcopal Church of St. Mary the Virgin, and the Metropolitan Life Tower. St. John the Baptist burnished his already stellar reputation. The AIA guide calls it "an exquisite single-spired brownstone church," with a white marble interior that "radiates light."

It was modeled on the thirteenth-century Reims Cathedral and employed the same French Gothic style as the Chartres Cathedral. Stained glass windows line

both aisles, and windows on the clerestory allow more light to flood the vaulted nave of the sanctuary, which can accommodate 1,200 people. Its bell tower is home to five massive bells weighing between 1,500 and 7,000 pounds.

Initially the church served families in what was a residential neighborhood but changed dramatically when construction began on Pennsylvania Station in 1904. Many blocks were razed to make way for the new transit hub and families were forced out. The mission of the church transformed from catering to German-speaking area residents to English-speaking railroad workers and then to a broader group of businesspeople and commuters. During this period, through the 1918 pandemic and two world wars, the church flourished.

And then came the 1970s when the city nearly went bankrupt and manufacturing jobs were disappearing from the city blocks. The finances of St. John the Baptist were ravaged as well, and by the early nineties the church was on the verge of collapse and faced permanent closure. But a major fundraising campaign saved it, and the church began an era of developing social programs for the poor and homeless. More misfortune befell the church when, in 1997, exactly 150 years after the original church burned, notes Brandes, a fire broke out and caused approximately $2 million in damage. Once again, the church rose from the ashes and by 2000, the building was restored.

In 2015, during the archdiocese's reorganization of New York parishes, St. John was joined with Holy Cross. While the latter caters to commuters pouring in and out of the Port Authority Bus Terminal, St. John the Baptist does the same for the equally vast sea of travelers arriving to and departing from New York's Pennsylvania Station.

St. John the Baptist

Church of St. Francis of Assisi

135 West 31st Street

Beauty and Pain

ROMAN CATHOLIC
BUILT 1890–92

In 1844 the pastor of St. John the Baptist on 30th Street, Father Zachary Kunz, a Hungarian Franciscan priest, found himself shut out of his own church. The closure was the result of a dispute with the parish's trustees and the bishop of New York ordered it closed. Unwilling to accept the idea of his parishioners being without a home, he petitioned the bishop to open a new church and soon purchased property nearby on 31st Street. That same year the cornerstone was laid by Bishop John McCloskey.

Forty years later, the congregation had outgrown its home and with a loan of $15,000 against a construction estimate of $60,000, the architect Henry Erhardt was commissioned to design the new church. It was completed in 1892. Newark's Archbishop Winand M. Wigger had grown up nearby and donated a large stained glass window dedicated to St. Francis.

By the turn of the century, what had been a suburban home for the church was transformed by urban development. The tranquil neighborhood became the city's notorious Tenderloin District, and the congregation lost a large number of parishioners. The parish, though, responded in innovative ways. To meet the needs of night workers, whether they were actors leaving the stage, newsroom staffers up against a deadline, or travelers grabbing a train from Penn Station, the parish inaugurated a "Nightworkers' Mass." Soon after, it offered a 12:15 P.M. mass and began hearing confessions throughout the day. During the Depression, the church offered a daily breadline which continues to this day.

St. Francis of Assisi continued to thrive and in 1961, three new marble altars were dedicated, ending a five-year period of construction and restoration. The grime was cleaned off the stunning "Great Mosaic" by Rudolph Margreiter and Joseph Wild, which was commissioned after World War II. Pictured in the mosaic is Mary

QUEEN OF THE ORDER OF FRIARS MINOR, PRAY FOR US

standing on the globe, encircled by seraphs and angels, with the Baby Jesus in one arm and a lily in the other.

The Church of St. Francis of Assisi holds a memory of the horrific September 11, 2001, attack on the World Trade Center. One of the church friars at that time was Father Mychal F. Judge, chaplain to the New York City Fire Department; he rushed to the scene and was the catastrophe's first official casualty. Millions saw the image of his ash-covered body being carried out of the rubble, which brought home the depth of the human tragedy that took place that fateful day.

Shrine and Parish Church of the Holy Innocents

128 West 37th Street

"The Actors' Church"

ROMAN CATHOLIC
BUILT 1869–70

OPPOSITE
The full glory of Constantino Brumidi's mural behind the altar was revealed under layers of dust and grime during a restoration project.

In 1870, construction was completed on the Church of the Holy Innocents, which was built for a congregation that formed in 1866. Cows still roamed the open pastures of the neighborhood, but it was soon to explode with development. The Gothic Revival church, in what is today's Herald Square area, was designed by the famed Catholic architect Patrick C. Keely.

Known as the actors' church, it served the thespians from the theaters that dotted the neighborhood. The great playwright Eugene O'Neill was baptized here. Worshipping alongside the theater crowd were the immigrants flooding the neighborhood. The various ethnic groups did not easily melt into the melting pot, and the ensuing mean streets gave the area its unaffectionate moniker: the Tenderloin District.

In the last decade of the century, James Gordon Bennett Jr., the son of the founder of the *Herald*, one of the city's top newspapers, made a daring decision and moved the paper away from "Newspaper Row," which was the nickname for Park Row. He chose what was then called Longacre Square. On a quest for newspaper supremacy, Bennett left behind his competitors Joseph Pulitzer, William Randolph Hearst, and others, who had purposely situated their publishing offices near City Hall. Bennett commissioned an extravagant building based on the fifteenth-century Venetian Renaissance Loggia del Consiglio in Verona. Designed by McKim, Mead & White, Bennett's edifice was built in 1894. Other newspapers followed, and in the early 1900s the area became known for its publishing. The theaters were pushed uptown, creating the Great White Way we know today.

The neighborhood changed again beginning around 1910, when the tenements were razed to make way for large commercial buildings. Textile companies and manufacturers laid the foundation for the thriving garment industry, and gave

"

SMALL CANDLES
$1.00

the area its moniker, the Garment Center (or the Fashion Center). Macy's built its world-famous department store that fills an entire block from east to west and north to south. Longacre Square became "Shopping Square" and was renamed Herald Square. Keely's magnificent church became obscured by the many buildings being erected.

Stepping inside the church, then and now, busy workers and commuters encounter both the literal and figurative sanctuary from the traffic, grime, and mercantile activity of the streets. Here one will find the venerated Return Crucifix. The large, lifelike statue "may be the most touched and most kissed Crucifix in New York," reads the church's website.

A magnificent mural, created by Constantino Brumidi, provides a glorious backdrop for the main altar. Born in Rome in 1805, Brumidi was admitted to the Academy of Arts in Rome when he was only thirteen years of age. In Rome his work adorns St. Paul's and the Loggia di Raffaello in the Vatican. But he was imprisoned for fourteen months during the French occupation of Rome. Upon release in 1852,

he fled to the United States. He quickly renounced his Italian citizenship, became an American citizen in 1857, and revered this country and its government. For some who have visited the US Capitol, his name may be familiar. Beginning in 1855, he made the building his canvas, creating paintings and frescoes for the President's Room in the Senate extension, the Senate corridors, and more. The Rotunda of the Capitol is bedecked with a frescoed frieze that portrays fifteen historical groups and is crowned by a gigantic frescoed canopy that measures more than 4,600 square feet.

He took up residence in New York where Father John Larkin, the first pastor of Holy Innocents, had "the foresight to engage this prominent Italian painter to create a monumental mural over the main altar," says the church's website. Over the course of the century, the original work became masked by layers of grime, varnish, and overpainting. But after a two-phase restoration effort—the first to stabilize and clean it, the second to remove the multiple layers of unoriginal materials—the work can now be seen in all its splendor.

Holy Cross Church

329 West 42nd Street

The "Saloon Priest's" Church

ROMAN CATHOLIC
BUILT 1854

Across the street from New York's Port Authority Bus Terminal, decidedly *not* known for its architectural aesthetics, sits a gem of a nineteenth-century Catholic church, Holy Cross. In the 1850s, tens of thousands of Irish Catholics escaped the overcrowded streets of Lower Manhattan and moved northward to the Times Square area, then known as Longacre Square and now as Hell's Kitchen. Protestants dominated the city, leaving few places in newer neighborhoods for Catholics to worship. Irish-born himself, Archbishop John Hughes created the church to serve these people. It was one of seventeen Catholic churches that Hughes created between 1840 and 1860.

In 1852, Archbishop Hughes appointed Father Joseph Anthony Lutz to lead the effort to build the church. Lutz, who became the first pastor of Holy Cross, at first serving his congregation in temporary quarters, oversaw fundraising for the building. The cornerstone was laid the same year. The pressing need for the church prioritized speedy construction over aesthetics, and the simple, seemingly solid brick Romanesque church opened in 1854. While lacking any ornate flourishes, the church nevertheless had a grandly imposing presence with its tall 160-foot spire towering over the modest buildings in the area. However, it wasn't quite as solid as it appeared. In 1867, the church was struck by lightning, and the ensuing fire caused serious damage. The building was discovered to be poorly constructed and could not be rebuilt. It was demolished, and a new Byzantine-style cruciform church built on the same site opened in 1868.

Like most of the churches at the time, as a way to raise funds to sustain them, pews had to be rented, or fees paid by those who sat in them. At some masses at Holy Cross, unskilled Irish immigrants paid five cents to sit in the galleries while Irish skilled laborers and professionals paid ten cents for pews, in addition to rent.

The Byzantine-influenced architecture is seen in the rear of the church.

The sanctuary provided a sharp contrast to the squalid living conditions of Hell's Kitchen and the frequent street brawls and ethnic conflicts. It is likely that parishioners from Holy Cross participated in the deadly draft riots of 1863 in the city's notorious Five Points neighborhood.

The pastor of Holy Cross from 1920 to 1932, Father Francis Duffy, had served as regimental chaplain for the Fighting Nineteenth in World War I and was considered a hero, gaining national attention and fame. He was a modern thinker who strove to reconcile "Americanism" with Catholicism, ideas that at times were in conflict with the archdiocese. According to Dr. Michael J. Pfeifer on the church's website, "prior to his appointment at Holy Cross, Duffy edited an innovative and liberal theological journal, the *New York Review*, which was shuttered by the archdiocese after Pope Pius X's 1907 condemnation of the heresy of 'modernism.'"

Duffy ministered to the nearby longshoremen as well as the workers at the local papers, including the *New York Times*, the *Daily News*, the *Daily Mirror*, and the *Herald Tribune*, who often labored deep into the night. To serve them, Duffy was granted a special dispensation from the Vatican to offer a very early Sunday mass at 2:30 A.M.

Succeeding Duffy was Monsignor Joseph McCaffrey, who presided over the church from 1932 to 1968 and for many years was simultaneously chaplain of the New York City Police Department. In 1943, in the midst of World War II, the

Victory Chapel in the lower church (now the basement) was opened. In his dedication ceremony, McCaffrey offered prayers for victory and peace and denounced "the philosophy of hatred and revenge," writes Pfeifer. More than fifteen thousand names of those serving were inscribed in the chapel during the war, with a gold star later placed next to the names of those who perished.

After the war, the opening of the Port Authority Bus Terminal and the burgeoning theater district brought new and different traffic into the church. Meanwhile, Times Square was at its seediest. Monsignor Robert Rappleyea, pastor in the 1970s and 1980s, was a catalyst for the revitalization and cleanup of Times Square and was chaplain of the Port Authority Police from 1975 to 1985. In 1995, another colorful priest, Father Peter Colapietro, took the helm. A former longshoreman born in the Bronx, he

Arms of the aisle and transept meet the dome

became known as the "Saloon Priest." He earned this moniker partly because he had worked in bars before he joined the priesthood, wrote James Barron in his 2018 obituary of Colapietro in the *New York Times*, and partly because he was a regular at Elaine's, the Upper East Side celebrity hangout that closed in 2011. Larger than life (literally—at six feet and 325 pounds), he served at Holy Cross for more than eighteen years, and was then transferred to St. Malachy's Roman Catholic Church for two years and finally to the Church of St. Monica on East 79th Street. His final mass at Holy Cross ended with a standing ovation and the accompaniment of bagpipes and drums from the city's Sanitation Department, for which he had been chaplain, Barron reported.

He once talked Mickey Rourke off a suicidal shelf and helped many other well-known celebrities who streamed in from the nearby theaters, restaurants, and bars. Stephen McFadden, a bar owner who knew Colapietro from Elaine's, told James Barron in an earlier feature he wrote for the *New York Times* that "focusing on smoking and drinking and all that stuff takes away from the essence of the guy. The essence, in a word, is goodness." McFadden said, "People would rather go to him than go to a shrink."

And he was forgiving. A two-hundred-pound statue of Christ was once stolen from the church and returned a week later. After the police dusted for fingerprints, Father Colapietro told them that the church would not press charges even if a suspect was found, explaining that the statue had been borrowed, not stolen.

In 2015, the Capuchin Order assumed care of Holy Cross, which was merged with St. John the Baptist on West 30th Street. Founded at the same time as Holy Cross, it served a German Catholic congregation where Father Lutz initially served. The merger links their early histories to bring them full circle.

Holy Cross Church   109

Church of St. Mary the Virgin

145 West 46th Street

"What's a Nice Church Like This
Doing in the Middle of Times Square?"

EPISCOPAL
CORNERSTONE LAID 1894

In 1833, John Keble, a priest and Oxford scholar, upended Episcopal thought when he gave a sermon at the University Church of St. Mary the Virgin in which he accused the Church of England of having lapsed into apostasy. Subsequently, along with his associates, Keble wrote "Tracts for the Times," which espoused that the Church of England (Episcopal in the United States) should return to its more Catholic roots. The group, known as "Tractarians," created an enormous brouhaha within the Church of England but had advocates on both sides of the pond, one of whom was Thomas McKee Brown. Ordained to the priesthood in 1866 by the sixth bishop of New York, Horatio Potter, Brown determined to bring his Tractarian theology to the Episcopalians of New York.

When Brown shared his vision with Potter, the timing was right—the bishop told him that a church was needed in Longacre Square (today's Times Square). Brown had another stroke of luck when John Jacob Astor offered to give him three lots on West 45th Street for the church with the stipulation that the "church should be free, and positively orthodox in management and working," according to the church's website. This meant that unlike most churches of the time in Manhattan, parishioners would not have to buy or rent pews.

The cornerstone of the original church was laid in 1868, followed by two years of fundraising to enable completion of the building. The church was dedicated in 1870, with Brown installed as rector. Brown immediately brought his Tractarian views to the fore. At the time, the traditional service of Episcopal churches was Morning Prayer, with the Eucharist celebrated only four times a year. Brown said, "It is the Mass that matters," and he brought daily celebration of the Eucharist to his congregation.

His orthodoxy had great appeal. By 1890, the congregation had outgrown its

+ To the Honour and Glory of God +
+ Sarah Elizabeth Murray + wife +
And in loving memory of +
Who entered into rest Sunday Dec + 11 + 1870 +
+ JESU MERCY + MARY PRAY +
+ MY SOVL + DOTH MAGNIFY + THE LORD +
+ AND MY + SPIRIT HATH + REJOICED IN + GOD MYL + SAVIOVR +
FOR HE + HATH REGARDED + THE LOWLINESS + OF HIS + HAND-MAIDEN

church and within two years, a wealthy parishioner passed away with fortuitous timing, leaving more than $700,000 to the church. Her bequest enabled the purchase of eight lots from 46th to 47th Streets, on the east side of Broadway. When the church arranged to return the land to the Astors, more luck came when William Astor, John Jacob's son, insisted on paying the church its market value of $76,000, even though the church had paid nothing for it.

Flush with funds, the trustees hired one of New York's leading architectural firms, Napoleon LeBrun & Sons, to design a French Gothic structure with the mandate that the interior be "lofty" and seat eight hundred persons. The plans included a rectory, clergy house, and mission house, presenting a challenge to fit it all on the allotted space. To accomplish the task, LeBrun suggested that rather than use massive stonework, they should employ a new, innovative method of construction using steel that could support the weight but create less bulk. The cornerstone for this edifice that still stands today was laid on December 8, 1894.

The nave is eighty feet tall from floor to ceiling and forty-six feet wide. Twenty-two stone piers line both sides of the nave supporting the clerestory. The forty-

eight-foot-deep chancel is adorned by the marble high altar that was moved from the original church. Its grandeur lent it its moniker, "the cathedral of Anglo-Catholicism." When the church opened—with admission by ticket only—the event was a sensation, attracting crowds that required police to manage, and grabbing headlines.

The Church of St. Mary the Virgin began its life in an area that was blossoming with theaters and home to a large residential population. It was a grand church in a nice little neighborhood. But by the turn of the century, the neighborhood was changing. Hotels and office buildings replaced residences and theaters. Further change came with the deterioration of the city during the sixties and seventies, bringing the grim seediness to Times Square for which it was known for decades. Adjacent was an even more disreputable and dangerous area known as Hell's Kitchen. Hence the church website's opening question: "What's a nice church like this doing in the middle of Times Square?"

Nevertheless, the parish prevailed, but it has come a long way from the Tractarian ethic. Today, the church proudly says, "Saint Mary's opens its doors to all people. . . . Our parish continues to redefine diversity and inclusiveness. We are families and single persons, young and old, gay, straight, conservative, liberal, and certainly a few who would define themselves as 'post labels,'" says the website. It has earned a new moniker, "Smoky Mary's," due to its frequent use of copious amounts of incense.

Church of the Sacred Heart of Jesus

457 West 51st Street

A Church in Hell's Kitchen

ROMAN CATHOLIC
CORNERSTONE LAID 1884

In 1876, as the population was moving farther uptown from Lower Manhattan, Cardinal McCloskey realized that "a parochial district was demanded by the growth of the city in that direction," according to the blog *Daytonian in Manhattan*. The Plymouth Baptist Church on West 51st Street was available and purchased by the parish. Meanwhile, the population growth in the neighborhood—and the congregation—was such that it soon became clear that the parish would need a larger space. By 1880, more lots on 51st Street were purchased and work began on the pastoral residence. In December 1883, sufficient funds had been raised to begin construction and plans for a larger church were announced by Father Martin J. Brophy, who headed the parish.

Brophy quickly commissioned the notable architectural firm of Napoleon LeBrun & Sons to design the building. LeBrun was well-known as the official architect of the New York Fire Department and as an ecclesiastical architect. For the Sacred Heart of Jesus, he built a Romanesque edifice with a sprinkling of Gothic and Moorish influences. The redbrick facade, trimmed with limestone and terra-cotta, protects the sanctuary, which seats 1,500. Upon the church's opening in 1885, the *Evening World* reported that "the appointments throughout are elegant and artistic, the interior of the church being one of the handsomest and most imposing in the city."

Its architectural grandeur would not protect it from several trials and tribulations over the years. As one of the largest Irish and German congregations of the city, the clergy recognized its potential political clout and, as the century was coming to a close, some priests began to use the pulpit to sway voters to vote Democratic, i.e., supporting the notorious Tammany Hall. The Republican candidate for state assembly, Lawrence P. Mingey, lost the election and wrote a letter of complaint to

Archbishop Corrigan, who denied any political affiliation. (Mingey was later convicted for check forgery.)

This acrimony was set against the rough, gritty, and dangerous neighborhood of Hell's Kitchen, where on February 27, 1906, a suspicious fire broke out in the church. In 1934, the church suffered two fires that happened within two weeks, both determined to also be of suspicious origin.

Later in the century, the church was once again under fire, this time from a best-selling book and movie. In *Sleepers*, published in 1995, Lorenzo Carcaterra's allegedly true story of his boyhood in Hell's Kitchen, the author portrays the church as the center of the brutal neighborhood and called its elementary school "uncaring." Leaders of the church were outraged and called the accusations defamatory. In the *New York Times*, the pastor, Reverend Kevin J. Nelan, said, "It's fake. Carcaterra's making an awful lot of money at the expense of the reputation of this church and people here. This is not exactly a genteel neighborhood. We have enough of our own rogues without making up any more." Further salt was poured on the wound when the book became a movie in 1996, starring Robert De Niro and Brad Pitt and directed by Barry Levinson.

The church has survived the fires, the political rancor, and the defamatory claims. Its stained glass windows have also survived, and they illuminate a far more tranquil sanctuary today.

St. Thomas Church

1 West 53rd Street

A Showstopper

EPISCOPAL
CORNERSTONE LAID 1911

As Manhattan's population grew, development moved northward. This geographical population shift, and the fact that transportation options were limited and slow, was the catalyst for the church's founding.

The first service of St. Thomas, on October 12, 1823, was held in a room at Broome Street and Broadway, a few blocks north of Canal Street, below which most churches and synagogues stood. At the time there were no railroads or streetcars. Within a few months, the congregation had been officially incorporated and a year later a cornerstone was laid at the corner of Broadway and Houston, farther north still. The relatively modest barnlike building, designed by Joseph R. Brady and Reverend John McVickar, showed hints of the Gothic masterpiece that would eventually house the parish. The edifice had typically Gothic pointed windows, battlements on its towers, and a trussed roof. Consecrated in 1826, it was destroyed by fire in 1851.

After weighing various options, the vestry decided it was best to rebuild on the same site and employed the firm of Wills and Dudley, who specialized in Gothic Revival churches. The second church was designed very similarly to the original. It was consecrated in 1852, but by 1857, the vestry was already contemplating another move. The last service was held at Broadway and Houston on Easter Sunday, 1866, and a lot for a new church was purchased at the corner of 53rd Street and Fifth Avenue.

The timing was right. The Gilded Age was born. Railroads crisscrossed the country; Carnegie, Morgan, Vanderbilt, and Rockefeller were amassing their fortunes, and the city had become the financial capital of the country. "Of the wealth that now flowed into the city of golden dreams, Saint Thomas was to have its good share," says Robert J. Wright in his history, *St. Thomas Church Fifth Avenue*, adding, "It is a painful fact that the ministry of the Episcopal Church, indeed most churches at this time, was directed to the socially privileged. Saint Thomas was no exception.

Pews were sold at public auction, openly advertised in the papers and sold to the highest bidders, who often paid considerable sums. Unsold pews were rented at substantial figures."

In 1865, Richard Upjohn was hired to design a church for the new Fifth Avenue location. His design for Trinity Church had made him the most renowned architect in the country. The cornerstone for St. Thomas was laid in 1868 for the Gothic structure that would soon support a magnificent 260-foot tower to dominate the avenue whose skyscrapers were yet to be imagined. Inside Upjohn's cathedral-like building, completed in 1870, was a chancel that Wright calls "a wedding of all the arts." The reredos featured a bas-relief of plaster finished in old gold depicting the *Adoration of the Cross by Angels and Cherubs* by the sculptor Augustus Saint-Gaudens. Murals painted by John La Farge flanked the bas-relief. It was perhaps the first example of *Gesamtkunstwerk* (a total work of art) in America.

While Upjohn's church stood in its splendor, its leadership set forth to address the great inequities in the city and founded a free chapel in a rented church at the corner of Prince and Thompson Streets. Worshippers were welcomed to services without having to pay fees for seating. This chapel became the first of three free chapels, along with others cropping up like the Church of the Resurrection on the Upper East Side, that, unbeknownst to those who proposed them, became the vision of the future. But it wasn't until November 5, 1961, that St. Thomas terminated the pew rentals.

Unfortunately, Upjohn's majestic church had a short life when once again a catastrophic fire destroyed the parish home. For the fourth time in its history, the parish of St. Thomas needed to build a new home. It was decided to build on the same site but to erect, in the meantime, a temporary chapel around which the new structure would be built.

The architectural firm of Cram, Goodhue and Ferguson was chosen with Cram, whose national reputation was beginning to blossom, at the helm. His vision was

The organ and pews dramatically framed from the balcony

one of Gothic integrity. "There will be no steel columns masked by applied stone, no girders doing the work supposed to be accomplished by vaults and arches. . . . From footings to crestings, it will be of such masonry as may be found in the most majestic buildings of the Middle Ages." Cram's exacting mandates included using limestone quarried in South Carrollton, Kentucky, sandstone from Wisconsin that is warmer and deeper in color, and custom-designed Guastavino tiles. All were obeyed. (Although later, steel had to be added to the north wall to keep it from collapsing.)

Opened in 1913 and completed in 1916, the edifice was 214 feet long, 100 feet wide, and its tower rose fifteen stories high. Above the entrance is an exquisite rose window that the *Architectural Record* called "beautiful and original, whose equal in tracery is hard to find even in the lovely windows of the old world." The distance between the nave and the columns is forty-five feet, and the height from the floor to the crown of the vault is ninety-five feet. Seating capacity is approximately 1,700. The space did not allow for transepts, however, so a parapet separates the nave from the chancel.

Cram's partner, Bertram Grosvenor Goodhue, was in charge of the detail and ornamentation of the church. He was responsible for the creation of what ultimately became, and remains, the pièce de résistance of the interior, the great reredos that some believe recalls that of Winchester Cathedral. At eighty feet tall and forty-three feet wide, it is one of the largest reredoses in the world from any period. Property lines did not allow for a window at this end of the church, nor are there chapels beyond the chancel, so the reredos defines "the liturgical east (geographical west) of the church," as Wright explains.

The Saint-Gaudens bas-relief reredos from the previous building had survived the fire and it was physically incorporated into the wholly new reredos design that still continued the central theme of the *Adoration of the Cross*. Also salvaged from the wreckage was the large gilt cross that adorned the altar and remains in use today. As he did throughout his career, Goodhue collaborated with sculptor Lee Lawrie, who carved the sixty individual statues of important biblical figures, prominent archbishops, and other leaders including George Washington. The parapet comprises eight panels of mosaics created with unpolished colored stones surrounded by ceramic tiles.

The interior is also home to other important works of art. One is a seventeenth-century Franco-Flemish tapestry, eight by fourteen feet, depicting Moses destroying the tablets of the law. The other is a circa 1640 painting attributed to Peter Paul Rubens and his school.

But finally Cram, Goodhue and Ferguson had burned through the budget and were out of money before the stained glass windows could be commissioned or installed. Much to Goodhue's chagrin, the temporary glass was glazed with simple painted geometric patterns for a price of only $7,000, for windows spreading throughout more than 9,500 square feet in area. It would be fourteen years before the first of thirty-four memorial stained glass windows in the main sanctuary were installed. The last one was installed in 1974. The windows were constructed with slab glass, thicker than the norm, and vibrantly colored. James Humphries Hogan, an American who designed the windows, blended Gothic with the then contemporary art deco style.

With its size, grandeur, and masterful architecture and design, St. Thomas is a showstopper.

St. Thomas Church

Fifth Avenue Presbyterian Church

7 West 55th Street

The Largest Presbyterian
Sanctuary in Manhattan

PRESBYTERIAN
BUILT 1873–75

OPPOSITE
Unlike many churches that have the organ in the rear of the nave, here it is above the altar, making it the focal point of this amphitheater-style sanctuary.

Fifth Avenue Presbyterian Church began its life in 1808 with twenty-six congregants on Cedar Street in Lower Manhattan. This small group comprised a remarkable range of the city's social hierarchy. Its early members included Oliver Wolcott Jr., a former secretary of the treasury; Betsy Jackson, a household slave; Richard Varick, George Washington's private secretary, who was to become a mayor of New York City; and Joanna Bethune, who founded the first "Sunday" schools for disadvantaged children.

The congregation grew quickly and moved three times until it settled in the gorgeous Gothic edifice that proudly still stands at the corner of Fifth Avenue and 55th Street. The building was designed by Carl Pfeiffer and was built from 1873 to 1875. It remains the largest Presbyterian sanctuary in Manhattan. The showstopping amphitheater style of the sanctuary and the balcony can seat 1,800 people. Yet even so, by the early 1900s, the church could not accommodate all the would-be worshippers and often had to turn away up to one thousand people on a given Sunday.

The exterior of the building is built with New Jersey red sandstone in a Victorian Gothic style. Inside, the sanctuary is a building within a building. None of its interior windows can be seen from the street. The sanctuary is notable for what it doesn't have—it has no right angles as the pews curve outward like a fan. This formation, along with sloping floors, allows clear sight lines to the front of the church. Also not here, with one exception, are representations of biblical figures or saints because, according to the church's website, there was "an iconoclastic austerity prevalent among nineteenth-century Presbyterians who believed no one should be venerated other than God." The exception is the woodcarving on the front of the pulpit that features the symbols of the four Gospel writers: Matthew (angel),

Mark (lion), Luke (ox), and John (eagle). Drawing attention to the pulpit aligns with
Reformed Protestant worship precepts that prioritize the spoken word.

The building-within-a-building structure had—and has today—the benefit of
blocking out noise from bustling Fifth Avenue and enabled the interior to control
its own climate. Pfeiffer's engineering prowess allowed highly advanced systems of
heating and cooling for the time. The smaller of the two towers, rising to a height
of 160 feet, contained air intakes powered by a seven-foot-diameter fan, allowing the air filling the interior of the church to be renewed every fifteen minutes,
as Robert A. M. Stern explains. Beneath the pews, wooden louvers allowed warm
air to rise from steam pipes in the basement, making chilly mornings of worship
much more pleasant. When New York's infamous hot and muggy summer days
were wearing down parishioners, gigantic blocks of ice were delivered to the basement, where fans blew the cooling air upward. Given that the sanctuary did not
install modern air-conditioning until 2003, this system must have worked remarkably well, although as the decades passed it would have become difficult to have the
iceman cometh.

The acoustical system was cleverly managed as well. The stenciled domed ceiling
is an aid, as well as the amphitheater-style pews, that together make it possible for
everyone in the vast theater to hear every spoken word, the choir, and the music
pouring from the seven-thousand-pipe organ.

Most of the carved woodwork that one sees today in the church is original. It was
designed by New York firm Kimbel & Cabus, who chose durable, light-colored ash
that has deepened in hue over the years. The thistle motif repeated throughout the
woodwork is meant as a tribute to the Scottish roots of Presbyterianism. Each post
of the pews is engraved with a quatrefoil.

Rising from the brownstone exterior 286 feet high is a steeple that, in 1875, was

Side view of the sanctuary highlighting the sweep of the theater-like pews

awarded the status of being the tallest in Manhattan. The bell tower, completed in 1876, houses the original clockworks that are still wound by hand every week. However, no chimes or peals of bells emanate from the tower—nor did they in the nineteenth century. At the time of construction, across the street sat St. Luke's Hospital (now the Peninsula Hotel), and there was concern that the ringing of bells would disturb the patients.

The exterior quiet didn't affect the goings-on within the sanctuary, which has a long tradition of memorable musical and social events. In 1910, Theodore Roosevelt Jr. was wed to Eleanor Butler Alexander with his father, the former president—and five hundred of his Rough Riders—among the guests. In 1965, Duke Ellington and his orchestra recorded *A Concert of Sacred Music*, and in 2009, 1,400 visitors poured into the church for a memorial for swing jazz dancer Frankie Manning.

A church house and an additional chapel were added to the grounds in 1825. These were designed by New York architect James Gamble Rogers, who trained at the École des Beaux-Arts in Paris and is best known for the Harkness Tower and Memorial Quadrangle at Yale University. Gamble was chosen by philanthropist Anna Marie Harkness, who donated 75 percent of the funds for the chapel and new church house.

The chapel, named the Kirkland Chapel in honor of Reverend Dr. Bryant M. Kirkland, who served as senior pastor from 1962 to 1987, was purposely designed on a much smaller scale than the main sanctuary, to make it more like a small parish church. The windows were designed by G. Owen Bonawit. Rendered in an art deco style, the windows on the south end portray Christ surrounded by seven archangels. At the north end, the four gospel writers, the twelve apostles, and other disciples are depicted.

Midtown East

Calvary Church

277 Park Avenue South

A Patrician Beginning

EPISCOPAL
COMPLETED 1848

OPPOSITE
*View of the Gothic Revival
sanctuary, with its soaring
ceiling and stained glass
windows above the
altar and organ pipes
flanking the chancel*

Calvary Church can claim a fine pedigree in both its many well-known parishioners and its architect, James Renwick Jr., one of the most esteemed designers of Calgary Parish. It was first organized in an 1836 frame church on Fourth Avenue. A decade later, it moved to its current location on Park Avenue South, across the street from the private, exclusive, and gated Gramercy Park. Calvary Church is privileged to be one of the thirty-nine buildings surrounding the park that is given keys for access.

Calvary is certainly not exclusive. Today's Alcoholics Anonymous (AA) can trace its roots to this church. During the tenure of Reverend Samuel Moor Shoemaker, who served at Calvary for twenty-eight years from 1924 to 1952, the church became the essential American headquarters for the Oxford Group (also known as the First Century Christian Fellowship). The international movement was founded by Frank Nathan Daniel Buchman, a Lutheran evangelist who, in 1938, instituted a campaign known as the Moral Re-Armament. The work toward personal and national spiritual reconstruction was conducted through "house parties," which were informal and intimate gatherings held in churches, homes, or educational institutions. At these gatherings, participants would share confessions and religious experiences with an emphasis on honesty, purity, love, and unselfishness. Practices involved "sharing our sins and temptations with another Christian; surrender our life past, present, and future into God's keeping and direction," and "restitution to all whom we have wronged directly or indirectly."

In 1935, the cofounders of Alcoholics Anonymous met and codified most of the Oxford Group's tenets for AA and its groundbreaking twelve-step program. One of the founders, Bill Wilson, wrote in *AA Comes of Age*, "It is through Sam Shoemaker that most of A.A.'s spiritual principles have come. Sam is one of the great channels,

132

one of the prime sources of influence that have gathered themselves into what is now AA." On its website, Calvary says, "The parish is proud of its connection to this program and continues to provide meeting space for AA groups each week."

Artists, writers, and musicians have loomed large in the church's history. Edith Wharton's family worshipped at Calvary, and it was here that the rector's daughter, Emelyn Washburn, introduced Wharton to Goethe, who became a favorite writer of hers. The church is featured in one of Wharton's most esteemed novels, the 1920 Pulitzer Prize–winner *The Age of Innocence*. In the book, Emelyn's father, Reverend Edward Washburn, was the model for the novel's character Dr. Ashmore.

One of only a few standout American Impressionists, Frederick Childe Hassam was a parishioner, and one of his works featuring the church is the 1893 painting

Calvary Church in Snow. The ninety-second mayor of New York City, a president of Columbia University, and a US diplomat worshipped at Calvary, as did Eleanor Roosevelt. Eleanor's parents, Elliott Bulloch Roosevelt and Anna Rebecca Hall, were married at the church in 1883. A couple of years later, in 1885, Eleanor herself was baptized in the sanctuary with her uncle, the future president of the United States, Theodore Roosevelt, as godfather.

Typical of his work, Renwick applied a refined Gothic Revival style to the church based on a French double-spired church design. In an early print of the church, two pointed spires soared skyward, but an 1865 photo, from the New York Public Library's collection, shows the church with two squared towers, minus spires. Now even those are gone, with only a stub of one tower remaining, and it does not show its original stonework. Its triple entrance, with red pointed arched doors within their arched stone frames, hints more toward the former Gothic elements of the church. The stained glass windows of the facade, and throughout the interior, also lend architectural authenticity and grandeur to the structure.

View of the glass-domed apse and the ribbed vaulting with medallions against a series of pointed arches

Our Lady of the Scapular

151 East 28th Street

From Munitions to Spiritual Medicine

ROMAN CATHOLIC
BUILT 1853–54 (CLOSED 2007)

Founded in 1889, the church of Our Lady of the Scapular was one of the many ecclesiastical Romanesque jewels that James Renwick Jr. built. "With Romanesque arches gushing like a fountain frozen in stone," says David W. Dunlap, the church is a most inventive work. Unfortunately, it fell prey to reorganization from the Archdiocese of New York and was closed in 2007.

At one time its rose window could be seen from the north side of the church on 29th Street, but it was covered over with masonry, which, in a way, benefited the interior. The windowless wall allowed the placement of a forty-six-by-twenty-six-foot Crucifixion created by Constantino Brumidi, who is best known for painting *The Apotheosis of George Washington* in the dome of the US Capitol building.

It was established by Carmelite friars who played a fascinating role in New York City's history. According to the *New York Times*, the Carmelites came to New York when Reverend Dr. Edward McGlynn, one of the city's most popular priests, was excommunicated after he supported a socialist candidate for mayor. The Irish immigrants were in an uproar over the excommunication, and the archdiocese's hope was that the arrival of the Carmelites would bring calm.

The subversive political activity didn't stop. The friars sheltered Irish revolutionaries on the run from British authorities, including Éamon de Valera, who became the first prime minister of the Irish republic. They guarded their munitions as well. The revolutionaries had amassed a cache of six hundred Thompson machine guns, wrapped in burlap sacks, that were hidden in the basement of the priory (then at 338 East 29th Street). The guns were intended to travel by ship to Ireland to aid in the War of Independence, but federal authorities seized them from the ship while still in dock in Hoboken, New Jersey.

But it certainly wasn't all war and politics at Our Lady of the Scapular. During

136

its heyday, its choir was renowned, attracting throngs of tourists, sometimes to the annoyance of the more devout worshippers. Less celebratory was the mission of the Irish Carmelite fathers who led the parish. For 118 years, the friars had ministered to the ailing and the dying in Bellevue Hospital, as well as offering daily mass for the health workers. In reporting on its fiftieth anniversary in 1939, the *New York Times* revealed that the church's friars made an average of eighteen thousand visits a year. The last priest at the parish before it closed, Philip Marani, arose at 5:00 A.M. every day and strode the few blocks from the rectory to the hospital. He made his last visit in June of 2007.

Our Lady of the Scapular   139

St. Patrick's Cathedral

625 Fifth Avenue

"America's Parish Church"

ROMAN CATHOLIC
CORNERSTONE LAID 1858

To see Paris, one must see the Eiffel Tower and Notre Dame; to see Rome, one must see the Colosseum and St. Peter's Basilica in the Vatican City; and to see New York, one must see the Statue of Liberty and St. Patrick's Cathedral. James Renwick's Gothic Revival masterpiece is more than an architectural marvel, more than the seat of the archdiocese, more than a place for Catholic worship. It is the city's soulful heartbeat as much as it is a monument to the heights to which poor immigrants have aspired—and reached.

In 1850, John Hughes, the fourth bishop and first archbishop of New York, conceived of a plan to build a grand cathedral on a prime block on Fifth Avenue, in the city's most fashionable neighborhood. It was a time when Catholics were the new immigrants, outsiders despised by the Protestant elites, the impoverished residents of the notorious Five Points tenement slums, and the politicians of the nativist Know-Nothing party. Around fourteen years earlier, at the original St. Patrick's Cathedral (page 56), which was then still the seat of the diocese, a vicious anti-Catholic mob attacked the cathedral. The church's surrounding wall, built in defense, still stands.

Hughes's wildly ambitious dream became known as "Hughes's Folly." Where would he procure the financial backing and public support to build a monument for a congregation of predominately poor Irish immigrants, against a backdrop of pervasive discrimination? Moreover, the site on Fifth Avenue was considered to be too far uptown to best serve the congregation. Hughes disagreed; he felt strongly that one day it would be, as he said, "right in the center of the city."

For thousands of years, "the center of a city was thought to be wherever its cathedral stood. The palace of a king might be grander, but it was universally considered to be of less importance than the house of God. If a king sat on a throne, so did a

140

bishop," Brendan Gill says. Hughes persevered and, one could say, doubled down on his "folly" when he hired the most prominent architect in the city, James Renwick Jr., to draw up plans to build what would be "one of the biggest [churches] in all Christendom," as Gill puts it.

The initial funding came from what was to become a decades-long series of innovative fundraising techniques by Hughes. First he approached "a group of leading Catholic gentlemen of the city" and secured pledges of $1,000 each from 101 of these men, along with two non-Catholics. He also asked the only slightly less well-off to donate $100 each, ultimately raising $70,000 in donations.

The cornerstone was laid on the Feast of the Assumption, August 15, 1858. There, Hughes defended himself against arguments that the money would be better spent going to the poor. How much better it was to give the working poor, the laborers, "honorable employment," rather than charity, by building the cathedral.

Hughes, proving himself to be a master at public relations, carefully orchestrated the ceremony for the laying of the cornerstone. He projected, according to former archbishop of New York Cardinal Terence Cooke, that in attendance would be "all the bishops of the province, in cape and miter, attended by their chaplains, one hundred boys in red cassocks, and surplices, priests, acolytes, St. Vincent de Paul members, and others who were to be part of the grand procession." Hughes wrote to the archbishop in Rome, Father Bernard Smith, of his intentions to produce "a sensation in this new country."

   MIDTOWN EAST

Hughes's hope had been to proceed continuously with construction until completion, but this was not to be. Just two years later, a lack of funds halted the work for what was hoped to be a brief period, but the Civil War commenced and construction ceased until the war was over.

By this time, Hughes was succeeded by Archbishop John McCloskey, who shared his predecessor's enthusiasm, and work recommenced apace. Twenty years later, with most of the exterior finished, there were still no interior furnishings or spires. To get to the finish line, McCloskey organized a fundraising extravaganza—the St. Patrick's Fair, which ran for a month. The *New York Times* called it "the grandest display of the kind that has been seen in the City since the great sanitary fairs of war times, when all New York gathered in the academy of music and passed out money like water for the soldiers."

With more than 1,400 volunteers and thousands showing up to peruse the array of tables, selling everything from gold and porcelain to furs and religious paintings, the first day was a scene of chaos. "By evening all was changed," reported the *New York Times*. "The light from 1,400 gas jets, streaming through the many stained glass windows of the marble pile, produced beautiful effects that were watched with delight by crowds of people in the street below. Within, the scene was one of marvelous beauty." Over twenty thousand people attended the opening night gala.

The elaborately carved wooden choir

The poor Irish themselves reached into their pockets for pennies, nickels, and dollars. Irish immigrant women, as opposed to some other groups, were allowed to work outside of the home. Most were servants in the great houses of the well-heeled. It was from these sparse pockets that St. Patrick's grew. In fact, a *New York Times* editorial chastised the city's Protestants for not sacrificing enough on behalf of the church. It read, "Even now, the noblest ecclesiastical building ever erected in this City, or in the United States, is slowly going up on Fifth Avenue, and where does the money for it come from? Largely out of the pockets of poor Irish servants, some of whom we have known to give as much as five or eight dollars a month out of their wages to this one special object."

Finally, in 1879, the same year that Thomas Edison demonstrated his incandescent light, the great cathedral was opened by Cardinal McCloskey. All was complete except the spires, which were finished in 1888. Rising 225 feet into the air, the spires are crowned by copper crosses.

Renwick's original plans for the interior did not have pews, but rather freestanding chairs, after the fashion of the cathedrals in Europe, but this was one of the few details not realized. Like the vast majority of churches at the time, funds were raised by the renting or buying of pews. Still ladened with debt, this became necessary for St. Patrick's. Of the 365 pews in the sanctuary, only 98 were free to sit in.

St. Patrick's Cathedral   143

By 1910, St. Patrick's was debt-free and was dedicated by Archbishop John Murphy Farley.

Most of what was in Renwick's stated plan was realized: the Gothic structure, the cruciform reflecting a Latin cross, the vast size, the two towers, the extensive use of marble that included marble steps to reach the entrance, and the masonry vault. His dream became a triumph. Renwick's two earlier commissions, Grace Church and the castle-like Smithsonian Institution building in Washington, DC, had garnered much acclaim, as did many of his later works, including St. Bartholomew's and All Saints Church (see pages 150 and 278). They can all be considered masterworks, but St. Patrick's Cathedral is Renwick's *Mona Lisa*. It is the one great masterpiece that will always be associated with his name.

The exterior is made of white, variegated marble from a quarry in Pleasantville, New York, in Westchester County, which was shipped to the site by a specially constructed branch of the Harlem Railroad. The mortar was chosen to match the stone so that the outside would appear as one continuous monolith. In a major $175 million repair and restoration project from 2012 to 2015, the biggest of several such projects over the years, conservators studied the original stone and went back to Westchester, where they found a quarry near to the original, this time in the village of Tuckahoe, in order to restore the facade to its gleaming original look.

The original doors were wooden, but in a 1949 restoration they were replaced with enormous regal bronze doors designed by Charles D. Maginnis. The figures that adorn the door were sculpted by John Angel. The doors were dedicated by Cardinal Francis Spellman on the one-hundredth anniversary of the Archdiocese of New York.

Renwick envisioned the interior to be made entirely of marble as well, but alas, once the walls had reached thirty feet high, the money for this expensive material ran out. Above thirty feet, the walls are a false marble stone. The vaulted ceiling is plaster, as is the ornamentation. The vast space inside matches the bright white of the outside.

The columns that line the aisles and nave as well as the high altar are made of marble. The high altar is adorned with an exquisite, shimmering bronze baldachin (canopy). The altar and baldachin are not from the original interior. It was felt that

the altar did not reflect the same degree of beauty as the rest of the cathedral, and in 1942 it was replaced with what we see today. The old altar was given to Fordham University's church, where it remains. Beneath the altar is a crypt, which holds the remains of the nine archbishops of New York, from Hughes to Egan.

Throughout the interior, which seats three thousand and can accommodate five thousand, are seventy-five stained glass windows that depict stories from the Old and New Testaments. One of the windows was a gift from Renwick himself. It depicts the architect giving the original plans to Cardinal McCloskey and Archbishop Hughes.

The music that pours from the cathedral's three organs has always been an im-

Chancel of a memorial side chapel

portant part of its history. Its nineteen copper, tin, and silver bells, ranging from 187 pounds to three tons, housed 160 feet above the ground in the north tower, peal for all New Yorkers. Its choirs have sung out throughout the decades. In the nineteenth century, the choir was made up of both men and women, but in 1903 that changed. The Vatican rejected classical and baroque music and insisted on Gregorian chants. Even more dramatic was the expulsion of women from the choirs, because, as the Vatican put it, women were not capable of being "ministers of the mass." It wasn't until 1968 when a woman sang in the cathedral again—for Robert F. Kennedy's funeral. Once more a mix of men and women, the choir has performed for heads of state and at the White House. In 2010 they traveled to the Vatican as the only choir from the United States invited to participate in the IX Festival Internazionale di Musica e Arte Sacra and performed, once again, for Pope Benedict XVI.

Beyond the beauty of the architecture, beyond the status of being the largest Catholic cathedral in America, is its role as our country's spiritual icon. It is sometimes called "America's Parish Church." His Eminence Timothy Cardinal Dolan, the archbishop of New York, said, "St. Patrick's Cathedral is a real symbol, to use a

Catholic word—a real sacrament for everything that is good and decent and noble and virtuous and enlightening and uplifting about New York."

While its marble arches have been home to many celebrations, it has also been where the funerals of venerated and historic figures have been held. Among them are the funerals of Babe Ruth, Ed Sullivan, Andy Warhol, and Senator Robert F. Kennedy. In this century, perhaps St. Patrick's most important role is the one it played in the aftermath of 9/11. It conducted countless back-to-back memorials for the police and firefighters who lost their lives in the destruction of the World Trade Center.

St. Patrick's Cathedral, called "a dream, an icon" by Cardinal Dolan, has been visited by four popes, including Pope Francis. It is visited by approximately five million worshippers, tourists, and seekers of solace each year. Its architectural splendor has endured for more than 140 years. Fordham University's Marcus Franz says, "Though St. Patrick's was built in [the] Gothic style, its design is original and distinct. The cathedral is noted for its purity of style, originality of design, harmony of proportions, beauty of material, and workmanship."

St. Patrick's Cathedral

St. Bartholomew's Church

325 Park Avenue

St. Bart's, Where Art Meets Worship

EPISCOPAL
BUILT 1917–19

St. Bartholomew's (known as St. Bart's to New Yorkers), like so many of the Episcopal churches founded in the first decades of the nineteenth century, had a humble first home in 1835 in a church at Great Jones Street and Lafayette Place. By 1872, the congregation had flourished and brought on James Renwick Jr., the "it" architect for grand religious edifices, who had by then won renown for Grace Church and St. Patrick's Cathedral. St. Bart's stood at the corner of Madison Avenue and 44th Street on land previously owned by William Vanderbilt. Later, a memorial to Cornelius Vanderbilt was added by way of a grand triple portal, designed by another acclaimed architect, Stanford White, who modeled it after what he believed to be the most beautiful work of architecture in France—the Abbey of Saint-Gilles-du-Gard, in the Provence region. White laid out the basic outline of the triple portal, which boasts bronze doors and friezes, but left the detailed design of the figures and decor to an array of venerable American sculptors. Herbert Adams created the left portal, Daniel French and Andrew O'Connor the central, and Philip Martiny the right. The frieze that connects the three arches was designed by O'Connor and shows the strong influence of Auguste Rodin.

In spite of its architectural pedigree, the Madison Avenue building suffered structural problems, and another distinguished ecclesiastical architect, Bertram Grosvenor Goodhue, was commissioned to design a new building on Park Avenue between 50th and 51st Streets. Cornelius Vanderbilt's wife, Alice Gwynne Vanderbilt, provided funds for her husband's memorial, still intact, to be moved to the new location. Goodhue went far beyond just using the triple portal as a jumping-off point for the design; "he brilliantly synthesized ancient and modern forms in a Byzantine-Romanesque style," according to David W. Dunlap.

Opened in 1918 and still standing today, the church not only is a place of worship

150

and community but also showcases the works of some of the most talented and innovative artists and artisans of the nineteenth century. Once through the majestic doors, one proceeds along a narthex that opens to a three-aisle nave. The traditional cruciform (cross) shape is supported by four arches resting on four large square piers. The nave, chancel, and transepts are barrel-vaulted, while the rough-surfaced coffee-hued tile that adorns the north and south walls is designed by the esteemed master builder Rafael Guastavino and his son. Along the north side, the capitals of the columns depict scenes from the Old Testament.

Among the stunning decorations of the interior is an apse that encompasses a half dome filled with a mosaic of glass and gold leaf depicting the Transfiguration. The extraordinary figures that can be seen from long distances from different vantage points within the sanctuary were designed by Hildreth Meière. Meière was a towering artist of art deco design who prevailed against the odds of succeeding in a man's world. She also designed the entrance lobby, and while she had to minimize art deco styling and motifs to create these traditional figures, as Celia McGee wrote in a New York Times article, "she got away with 'The Six Days of Creation,' in full-blown art deco." Later, between 1948 and her death in 1961, she also designed three sets of three stained glass windows. Meière was both a muralist and mosaicist whose rare talent couldn't go unnoticed, and she often collaborated with both Goodhue and Guastavino.

Another dynamo of the architectural design scene of the late nineteenth and early twentieth centuries was Lee Lawrie, a sculptor whose work can also be seen in St. Bart's. He sculpted the four marble prayer stands in front of the windows (originally placed in the chancel). Another of Lawrie's creations is the lectern, which is carved with the symbols of the evangelists, one in each corner, depicting the winged man, the ox, the eagle, and the lion. The lectern is built into a parapet wall of Sienna marble that is decorated with mosaics.

While this hybrid of Romanesque and Byzantine styles emanates beauty and artistry inside and out, ugliness came to the church in the form of an existential battle for the building itself that erupted in the 1980s. On the block that St. Bart's occupies, the sanctuary sits on the northern half; the southern half houses a still very active community house, garden, and currently a café. The idea for the garden goes all the way back to 1915. In a January 16, 1915, article in the *Architect* titled "The Proposed

ABOVE
Hildreth Meière's majestic mosaic of the Transfiguration

LEFT
The chancel of a side chapel

New St. Bartholomew's," Goodhue wrote, "This church, like all our other churches, whatever their style, should possess more space than our great American cities permit. It should not be elbowed and jostled by great apartment houses, but should rise through the greenery of trees and flowers." It is astonishing that the open area remains as an oasis in Manhattan's precious real estate, but it almost wasn't so.

In 1981, a real estate developer offered to build an office tower on the site of the community house and garden from which the adjacent church would reap tremendous financial benefit and security. The parish was acrimoniously divided by the proposition, which also involved conflict between the church and the city's historic preservation movement. The building had already been designated a landmark in 1967 by New York City's Landmarks Preservation Commission. The battle went on for over a decade, wending its way through the court system until 1991 when the Supreme Court declined to hear St. Bartholomew's appeal of the Second Court decision that favored the Landmarks Preservation Commission, thus preventing the office tower's construction. In 2016 it was designated a National Historic Landmark.

The ceiling features hand-carved wooden ornamentation where the tiled ceiling of the nave and transept meet.

Central Synagogue

652 Lexington Avenue

The Oldest Synagogue in
Continuous Use in New York City

REFORM JUDAISM
CORNERSTONE LAID 1870

On the occasion of Central Synagogue's 140th anniversary, three congregants—Stella F. Fuld, Janet Stone, and Mildred Ross—authored a special publication, *Central Synagogue: 140 Years.* In it, Clara Schwarzkopf Benjamin recounted the story of her grandfather, Leopold Schwarzkopf, whom she describes as "a handsome young man" of seventeen who fled from Bohemia to avoid conscription in the army. After establishing himself in New York, he invited a group of fellow Bohemians to his home on Lewis Street to explore the idea of forming a synagogue. And so they did, founding Congregation Ahawath Chesed (Love of Mercy) in 1846, the foundation for Central Synagogue, the oldest synagogue in continuous use in New York City.

In 1846, the group of eighteen Bohemians (in Judaism, eighteen, "chai," is a "good luck" number) consecrated the nascent congregation in Coblenzer's Hotel at 69 Ludlow Street. As it expanded, the congregation made a series of moves to accommodate its growing membership, including the purchase of a remodeled church on the corner of 4th Street and Avenue C. It was here the congregation decided that it was time for a permanent rabbinical staff and hired Dr. Adolph Huebsch and Samuel Welsch from Bohemia to serve as rabbi and cantor.

Rabbi Huebsch set the tone for the liberalism that remains a vital part of the synagogue today. Huebsch reformed and moderated traditional orthodox traditions, believing that the services needed to be "in harmony with the conditions and requirements of modern times," as Fuld et al. wrote, and that "He believed that his congregation could not be truly consecrated until it became part of New York City and America." Huebsch developed a new prayer book that was widely adopted in the city and around the country, and he championed the idea that there was a need for service to both the religious and secular communities. He demon-

156

strated this by encouraging congregants to participate in post–Civil War recovery programs.

Two decades later, the congregation, now with 140 families, had outgrown its 4th Street home, bought property on 55th Street and Lexington Avenue, and hired Henry Fernbach, one of the most prominent Jewish architects in the United States, to design it. The cornerstone was laid on December 14, 1870, and the building completed in 1872. The original gas-burning eternal light remained illuminated until it was converted to electricity in 1946.

Unlike most synagogues, Central faces to the west, the opposite of the tradition in which synagogues are oriented to face Jerusalem. Apparently the real estate deal was too good to pass up and the congregation decided it was best to have the entrance on Lexington.

Fernbach was tasked with building a sanctuary with seating for 1,400 people, a giant leap of faith for the congregation, considering the modest size of the membership at that time. In 1898, Central Synagogue merged with another congregation, Shaar Hashomayim, which filled many of the pews. The synagogue was renamed Ahawath Chesed Shaar Hashomayim and in 1918 renamed itself Central

Central Synagogue   159

Synagogue. Today, with 2,600 families and members, the mandate for a large sanctuary proved a prescient one.

Fernbach employed a style rife with Moorish architectural characteristics, in order to give it a distinct look from the many Christian churches dotting the city. The entire exterior features contrasting dark and light stones in bands across the walls and within the arches, creating an almost chiaroscuro effect as the lighter stones draw the eye to dappled light. Two sentinel towers stand tall, crowned with copper globes of which the celestial blue grounds the gilt ornamentation. Golden Stars of David encircle each globe, which sparkles with stars above and below the intricately adorned diameter. The pièce de résistance are the minarets that elegantly top the towers. The crenellated towers and facade afford it a castle-like gravitas. The towers were modeled after the Dohány Street Synagogue in Budapest.

At the entry are triple Moorish stone arched doors, enhanced by three miniature rose windows that serve as a stage for the much larger magnificent rose window above. When it was designated a landmark, the NYC Landmarks Preservation Commission called it "the finest example of Moorish Revival architecture in New York City."

In 1998, this majestic landmark fought to survive when a devastating fire did

tremendous damage to the interior, including collapsing the roof and some support beams and destroying the choir loft and organ. The timing of the fire has a bit of a silver lining—it happened in the final stage of a three-year renovation project, so precious ritual objects, including the Torah scrolls, had been removed from the construction site and were saved. And a new discovery was made: three six-foot-square stained glass panels that had been hidden for decades were uncovered and restored and now bathe the ark in colored light. The glass roundels of the two-story stained glass windows were salvaged from the fire and dedicated to the firemen whose heroic work allowed the synagogue to continue its long life.

The interior matches the grandeur of the exterior with the richly hued patterns that are stenciled and hand-painted on surfaces throughout the sanctuary. After the fire, the stenciling was redone by hand. Slender cast-iron columns connected by an arched architrave separate the nave from the two aisles on either side. The extravagantly decorated columns are intricately carved and are crowned with gilded capitals.

For the floor, Fernbach ordered many thousands of encaustic tiles from England that he alternated with diamond-shaped brown quarry tile with extensive additional detailed patterns and borders. The floor was destroyed in the fire; remarkably, the synagogue had the original blueprints *and* the English company was (and is) still in existence, so tens of thousands more tiles were reordered and the floor reconstructed.

The woodwork on display in the ark and other parts of the synagogue was done by the same company that made furniture for the White House. Pottier & Stymus, whose factory was nearby on 42nd Street and Lexington Avenue, constructed furniture for President Ulysses S. Grant's office, the Cabinet Room, and the secretary of the treasury's office.

Central Synagogue

Upper West Side

Church of St. Paul the Apostle

405 West 59th Street

Divine Artistry

ROMAN CATHOLIC
CORNERSTONE LAID 1876

The Church of St. Paul the Apostle was the vision of Reverend Isaac Thomas Hecker, who in 1858 founded the Missionary Society of St. Paul the Apostle, commonly called the Paulist Fathers. His dreams were on a grand scale. According to the church's website, he hoped to build a noble basilica that would combine the artistic ideals of the past with the American genius of his day. Indeed, for a time, the church was the second largest in the nation, topped only by St. Patrick's Cathedral.

The gray granite of the exterior was salvaged from the embankments of the Croton Aqueduct on the Upper West Side, the Croton Reservoir at 42nd Street and Sixth Avenue (now Bryant Park), and other structures throughout the city. In its austerity, the gray exterior is commanding, if not foreboding, while the interior is anything but, with works from several of the most preeminent artists from the nineteenth and early twentieth centuries including John La Farge, Lumen Martin Winter, Stanford White, and Bertram Grosvenor Goodhue.

A year after it was founded, a simple brick church was built and was quickly outgrown by the parish. The initial design and construction of the edifice that realized Hecker's ambitions, begun in 1876, was the work of the architect Jeremiah O'Rourke. By the early 1880s, the project had been taken over by George Deson, who was a Paulist priest trained at West Point as a military engineer.

The style of the church blends Medieval Gothic and Romanesque influences. Its website attributes its inspiration to fourth- and fifth-century early Christian basilicas in Ravenna, Italy, while the NYC Landmarks Preservation Commission suggests that Hecker's model may have been the thirteenth-century Basilica of Santa Croce in Florence, Italy.

164

Stained glass windows were added over time but the earliest, unveiled in 1885, is Our Lady of the Angels—the fourth-largest stained glass window in the world. The three that are larger are found in the Cathedral in Milan. The outer windows in the chancel were designed by muralist and stained glass designer John La Farge, who also designed the marble baptistry. Beyond his own artwork, La Farge acted as an overseer of all aspects of the decoration of the church from 1884 to 1889.

The golden dome of the baldachin (the canopy above the altar) was designed by Stanford White and is supported by six marble pillars with gilded Corinthian capitals. In front of one of the interior's chapels, St. Patrick'S Chapel, stands the Bruges *Madonna*, a bronze sculpture created by Michelangelo. It is a positive copy of the original that was made with permission of the Belgian government and cast by the Gruet foundry in Paris. It is one of two copies that exist in the world, the second of which is in St. Cuthbert's in Edinburgh.

Goodhue's contribution is the round mosaic made of marble that is on the floor at the church entrance. The sculptor Lumen Martin Winter is responsible for the striking blue and white bas-relief that extends sixty feet in width over the main entrance. Composed of Roman travertine stone and venetian glass tesserae, it lends the facade its only colorful and ornate feature. Winter also sculpted the Botticino marble statue of *The Angel of the Resurrection*, beneath which lies the tomb of Father Hecker.

Congregation Shearith Israel

8 West 70th Street

"The Spanish and Portuguese Synagogue"

ORTHODOX JUDAISM
BUILT 1896–97

OPPOSITE
The marble ark is
open to reveal a pastel
array of Torahs.

Congregation Shearith Israel, the first synagogue in North America, which stands today on Manhattan's Upper West Side, is rooted in a history that goes back more than three and a half centuries. From a humble rented space to its current stately Greco-Roman structure, Shearith Israel has undergone many physical incarnations and addresses, until the cornerstone was laid for the latter building in 1896.

Its history begins in September of 1654 when twenty-three Jews, mostly Spanish and Portuguese, arrived in New York from Recife, Brazil. They did not get a warm welcome—Governor Peter Stuyvesant did not want Jews in New Amsterdam. These brave souls fought for their rights and, in 1655, won permission from the Dutch West India Company to remain in the colony. However, that permission did not include the right to worship publicly. According to a quote on the synagogue's website, the Jewish community was very small and was allowed to only worship "in all quietness within their houses," although land for a cemetery was granted in 1656.

When British rule succeeded the Dutch in 1664, the repressive legislation was repealed, but not immediately. It wasn't until 1700 that the first group of Jews rented a space on Mill Street (now South William Street). Three more decades passed, and finally, in 1729—seventy-five years after the twenty-three Jews emigrated from Brazil—the first synagogue in North America was built and Shearith Israel was founded. The significance of its origins are honored today by its common moniker, the "Spanish and Portuguese Synagogue" and by the fact that the original building is still known as the "Mill Street Synagogue."

The congregation followed Sephardic ritual. Sephardic Jews refers to those who originally were from Portugal, Spain, the Middle East, and Northern Africa;

Ashkenazic refers to those Jews who have European roots, primarily eastern Europe and Germany. While most synagogues throughout the world were either Ashkenazic or Sephardic, the Shearith synagogue was home to both, even when the former became the majority group. Hyman Grinstein, in his book *The Rise of Judaism in New York*, speculates that the acquiescence of the Ashkenazic was motivated by a desire to maintain a united Jewish community or, perhaps, the Ashkenazic were too poor to establish a synagogue of their own. The unity didn't last. In 1825, the more recently arrived Ashkenazic with English, Dutch, German, and Polish backgrounds seceded to form their own congregation, B'nai Jeshurun.

This was the first of many further secessions, crowning Congregation Shearith Israel as the mother of most synagogues in New York. Another example is Rodeph Shalom, which was founded when a group of German Jews withdrew from Shearith in 1842. "Indeed, the story of congregations in New York, until 1860 at least, is one long account of secession and more secession," Grinstein writes. Only a very few were founded by new immigrant groups.

Besides the ritual differences between the Ashkenazic and the Sephardic, there was a desire to worship alongside those who hailed from the same country, city, town, or village in Europe with each hyperlocal group practicing its own variations in rituals. As the Jewish population increased and evolved, synagogues were often sold from one congregation to another.

The building on Mill Street was in use for nearly a century. By 1817, the building was completely dilapidated and rebuilt. But just like the rest of the city's population, Jews were moving uptown, precipitating the sale of the Mill Street Synagogue and allowing the construction of a new synagogue on Crosby Street—the first of several moves. In 1860, the congregation moved farther uptown to 19th Street and finally to its current home which was built from 1896 to 1897. The building was designed by the architectural firm Brunner & Tryon. The team based their Greco-Roman design on ruins found in Galilee to gain what Arnold W. Brunner called the "sanction of antiquity." The limestone facade features four grand Corinthian columns.

Within the building are two sanctuaries, of which the smaller is known as the "Little Synagogue." Remarkably, in that space, some of the furnishings from the original Mill Street Synagogue are in use today—fitting for a synagogue whose name means "remnant of Israel." The temple is also home to Torah scrolls that were desecrated by British soldiers during the Revolutionary War.

For more than one hundred years, until 1825 when B'nai Jeshurun was established, Shearith Israel was the one and only synagogue in New York City—a stunning fact. After 1825, through further fissures, the number increased quickly. By 1855, there were more than twenty synagogues in Manhattan.

Church of
the Blessed
Sacrament

152 West 71st Street

From Hay to Italianate Splendor

ROMAN CATHOLIC
CORNERSTONE LAID 1887

In 1887, when the Upper West Side of Manhattan was still a rustic countryside, Henry Osborne Havemeyer's stable stood on the north side of West 72nd Street. On April 10 of that year, Father Matthew A. Taylor, the first pastor of Blessed Sacrament, celebrated the first mass of Easter Sunday on a makeshift altar in the stable. Three months after this service, the ground was broken on 71st Street, just west of the church's current site, for a redbrick Italianate building, which opened its doors on Christmas of the same year and was built to hold eight hundred people. A month later, Archbishop Corrigan dedicated the church.

Only twenty years later, the congregation had outgrown its home, and in 1917, it was torn down to make way for a bigger home of worship. A thirty-seven-year-old graduate of Columbia University School of Architecture, Gustave Steinback, won the commission. For his design, he harked back to Sainte-Chapelle in Paris, a small Gothic chapel built by Louis IX in the 1240s to house relics from the Holy Land.

A passerby would have been awestruck by the looming magnificence of the church, towering over the sparsely developed land. Over the years, while the dimensions haven't changed, the church has been swallowed up by its towering neighbors. Even as early as 1922, when the church sold its Broadway parcel to the developers of the Hotel Alamac, its physical stature and visibility diminished in proportion. One need only narrow their peripheral vision to be overwhelmed by this midblock masterpiece.

Over the main portal is a tympanum (the area between the lintel over the doorway and the arch) that artistically connects the church to the Vatican. The carved relief recalls Raphael's fresco *The Triumph of the Eucharist* (*The Disputation of the Sacrament*). It is the companion piece to Raphael's *The Triumph of Philosophy* (*The School of Athens*), which depicts Plato, Aristotle, and other Greek philosophers

172

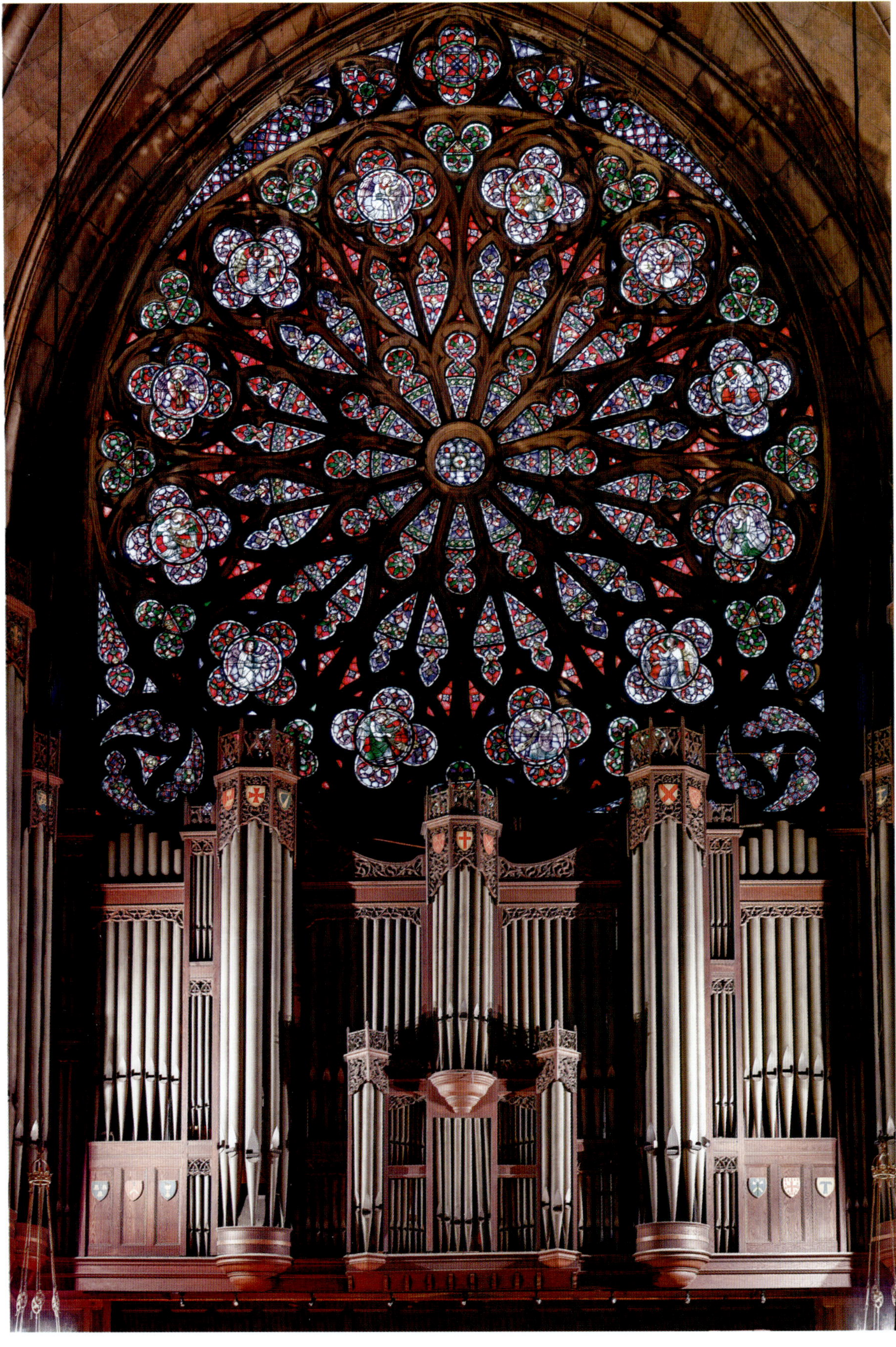

debating at the Acropolis. The pair of frescoes honors the twin medieval sciences of theology and philosophy and were created by Raphael around 1509.

The top of the lunette features a carving of God the Father with Christ and Mary, St. John the Baptist, and the Holy Spirit in an aureole below. Elaborate statuary and carvings adorn other parts of the exterior on the upper tower and side doors.

A spectacular rose window adorns the area above the entrance. It was designed by Clement J. Heaton, a stained glass maker and thirteenth-century art expert whose windows adorn cathedrals and churches throughout Europe and the United States. Hailing from England, he abandoned his father's glass firm and went to Switzerland for thirty years where he produced stained glass. He came to this country at the behest of renowned church architect Ralph Adams Cram (who designed St. Thomas Church, the Church of the Transfiguration, and the Cathedral of St. John the Divine) around 1912 and set up his own workshop and glass kiln in West Nyack, New York. In addition to the rose window, Heaton made seven windows lining the aisle of the soaring nave and six clerestory windows.

Church of the Blessed Sacrament   175

West End Collegiate Church

245 West 77th Street

A Church for New Amsterdam

DUTCH REFORMED PROTESTANT
CORNERSTONE LAID 1891

West End Collegiate Church is part of the Collegiate Reformed Protestant Dutch Church in the city of New York. The term "collegiate" dates back to 1652 when the duties of Minister Johannes Megapolensis became too much for one person and the assistant who joined him was known as a colleague; "collegiate" sprung from there. Building began in 1891, using a bit of millstone from the original seventeenth-century gristmill which to this day can be seen in the vestibule of the charming West End Collegiate Church.

With the rapid development, the area became a hodgepodge of architectural styles, drawing criticism. Developers were urged to bring more uniformity of style to the area. The premier architectural firm of McKim, Mead & White wanted to attract the upper echelon—the old money—and felt that a sense of history must be incorporated into the new neighborhood. Wanting to avoid the Romanesque style that they deemed was overused, they chose a revival of the Dutch Colonial style.

The architect for the church, Robert W. Gibson, needed no persuasion—he styled the church after the 1606 Vleeshal in Haarlem, the Netherlands.

The exterior features brown brick with terra-cotta ornamentation. Inside, the octagonal pulpit rests upon a carved oak base. The Dutch Colonial style is particularly apparent in the carved oak pulpit chairs. Rounded arched windows and the rounded arches of the colonnade reveal Romanesque elements of style. The stained glass windows, three of which are from the Tiffany studios, were added over the years.

First Baptist Church

265 West 79th Street

The First Baptist Church
in New York City

BAPTIST
BUILT 1890–93

Welcoming the hordes of folks descending or ascending the grimy stairs of the 79th and Broadway subway station is the First Baptist Church on the northwest corner, standing proudly at an odd angle; it is set forty-five degrees to the street, kitty-corner if you will. The parish was organized in 1745 when thirteen people gathered to worship in the home of Jeremiah Dodge. After temporarily worshipping in a rigging loft on William Street, the congregation bought a lot at 35 Gold Street and erected a church. The first service was held there on March 14, 1760, and the church was officially established as "The First Baptist Church of New York," with John Gano as its first pastor.

The number of parishioners expanded quickly, from twenty-seven to two hundred in only three years. Gano clearly was gaining popularity, but when the Revolutionary War commenced, his ministry was interrupted when he left to serve as chaplain to General George Washington. It is believed that Gano baptized Washington—at the future president's request—at a military camp in Newburgh, New York. When he returned from the war, the congregation came together once again under his leadership. Later in his career, Gano helped found Brown University.

The original church, desecrated during the Revolutionary War, was replaced with a new one on the same street and subsequently moved again to the corner of Broome and Elizabeth, where a Gothic Revival building was erected. After the Civil War, the area was becoming more commercial than residential, so again the church moved, in 1871, to Park and 39th. Finally, after surviving two wars, the church relocated to 79th and Broadway.

For the design of the Upper West Side location, a competition was held, with George M. Keister winning the commission, although his earlier projects were primarily for theaters and residential properties. Construction began in 1890 and was

THAT FORM OF DOCTRINE
DELIVERED YOV = BVRIED
IN BAPTISM WHEREIN ALSO
YE ARE RISEN WITH HIM
ΕΝ ΑΡΧΗ
Ο ΛΟΓΟΣ
HYMNS
RESPONSIVE READING
SCRIPTURE LESSON

completed in 1893. The exterior is built from limestone that rests on a granite foundation. Besides the quirky angle of the church's footprint, it is crowned with an odd assortment of unequal towers. The main arched entry is crowned by two towers: one square, spired, and tall; the other round, squat, and topped with a gazebo-like edifice, lending it an unfinished look. The taller is believed to represent Christ as the head of the church; the shorter symbolizes that the church will remain incomplete until the return of Christ. The north and south sides of the building are topped with lower spired towers.

The cornerstone is inscribed with the monogram "FBC" (First Baptist Church); the Greek letters chi and rho, the first two letters of the name of Christ; and the letters alpha and omega, the first and the last letters of the Greek alphabet, used as a title for Christ in the Scriptures. Originally the four corners of the upper auditorium bore Stars of David to show that "the Gospel was to be taken from the four corners of the earth, to the Jew first and also the Greek" (Romans 1:16).

Way back in the early days of the church, when it was in its second home on Gold Street, the parishioners behaved atrociously in their treatment of a group of African visitors. That group went on to form the Abyssinian Baptist Church, which is one of the most important Black Baptist churches in the country (see page 286). And George M. Keister, ironically, twenty years later, went on to design the Apollo Theater, which opened in 1913 and for over a century has been an architectural and cultural landmark in Harlem and for the African American culture at large.

Holy Trinity Catholic Church

213 West 82nd Street

The Hagia Sophia of New York

ROMAN CATHOLIC
CORNERSTONE LAID 1900

The first home of Holy Trinity was steps away from Grand Central Terminal and was a "work church for working people," said Montgomery Schuyler, a nineteenth-century architecture critic. Built from 1871 to 1874, it was an impressive Gothic-inspired building, in which the interior space was in the form of an ellipse, allowing excellent acoustics. The designer, Leopold Eidlitz, conceived the church as "a theater with ecclesiastical details."

By the end of the century, the area surrounding Grand Central became predominantly commercial, and in 1898, a new parish on the West Side was established, with Holy Trinity to follow uptown. Construction didn't commence until 1900, when Father Considine resolved to construct a church whose "beauty would be an inspiration to man and a tribute to God." To fulfill his vision, he hired Joseph A. McGuire as chief architect. McGuire took an atypical approach, eschewing the predominance of Romanesque and Gothic structures, and harking back to the church of Hagia Sophia built in Constantinople (now Istanbul) in AD 537 and considered the birth of Byzantine architecture. Some refer to it as the Hagia Sophia of New York, but others see the famous Oyster Bar at Grand Central as a fair comparison as well. One unhappy critic, in an article on the church's website, posits that it does not compare to other Byzantine churches by saying, "Both in its interior and exterior, for example, one can note disturbing similarities to the elephant house of the Bronx Zoo." Back in 1912, the *Catholic News* was kinder in its assessment: "The new Church of the Holy Trinity . . . is built of brick and terracotta and possesses a handsome facade [and] is considered to be one of the finest examples of Byzantine architecture in this country."

The facade features the characteristic Byzantine use of gold adornments, which are found on either side of the rose window and elsewhere. Four pairs of imposing

bronze doors provide entry to the sanctuary, where geometric patterns, mosaics, and multicolored marbles are also hallmarks of Byzantine design. Rising above the nave is a huge dome constructed with Guastavino tiles. A pantheon-like oculus, covered by a skylight, is at the center. A baldachin (a marble covering) partially encases the altar and is supported by four pillars that continue the Byzantine motif. Luminous mosaics adorn the sanctuary, although they do not cover all the walls as one would find in a medieval Byzantine structure.

Hanging from an arch on the east side of the church is a twelve-foot bronze crucifix that differs from modern representations of Christ. Between 700 and 1100, Christ was depicted not falling forward from the cross in an expression of suffering, but attached to the cross and appearing strong and composed. Small stained glass windows throughout the church minimize light and envelop the sanctuary in an air of mystery and somberness.

OPPOSITE
*Marble stairs leading
to the pulpit*

ABOVE
*The petal stained glass
window shines light on
the organ and loft.*

Congregation Rodeph Sholom

7 West 83rd Street

From Orthodox to Reform

REFORM JUDAISM
BUILT 1929–30

OPPOSITE
The ark, seen here open with its collection of Torahs, is set against wooden panels with detailed fretwork containing a series of Stars of David.

The Congregation of Rodeph Sholom is one of the oldest in New York, founded in 1842 by eighty German immigrants who first gathered on Attorney Street. The eighty quickly grew to 189 members and a larger space was found on Clinton Street in 1850. Then in 1891, following the residential migration uptown, the congregation moved into an even larger space at Lexington Avenue and 63rd Street. In 1930, with many members moving into gracious apartments on the Upper West Side, the congregation moved for the last time to its current home on West 83rd Street.

The Romanesque building was designed by Charles B. Meyers. Construction began in 1929—a bold, confident move, given that the Depression was underway. It was completed in 1930 and dedicated on the Jewish holiday of Purim in March of that year.

Originally an Orthodox temple, over the years it transitioned to Conservative rituals and finally to Reform Judaism in 1901. The changes were in play early on, when in 1844 the first rabbi of the congregation left because he didn't think that it was necessary for women to wear sheitels (wigs). In 1875, under Rabbi Aaron Wise—the father of Stephen Wise, who became an important Jewish leader—the congregation was rededicated with Conservative services, including using a choir and organ for the first time and conducting some sermons in English, not German as they had been. In 1899, men no longer had to wear hats and the observance of the second day of Rosh Hashanah was abandoned. In 1924, the synagogue adopted the Union Prayer Book, completing its transition to Reform Judaism.

For its anniversary celebrations, Rodeph Sholom has attracted renowned speakers and politicians. For its one-hundredth anniversary in 1942, presidential candidate Wendell Willkie was a guest speaker. The celebration of its 125th anniversary

186

was held at the Plaza Hotel with Senator Jacob Javits and Rabbi Maurice Eisendrath, president of the Union of American Hebrew Congregations, in attendance. And in 2006, when Robert N. Levine was elected president of the New York Board of Rabbis, Senator Hillary Rodham Clinton gave the opening remarks at his installation in the main sanctuary.

In 1970, Congregation Rodeph Sholom established the first Reform day school in North America. It began with only kindergarten and first grade and has grown since, now accommodating kindergarten through eighth grade. In 1977, the school moved into a new building on West 84th Street that adjoins the synagogue.

The design of the synagogue combines a mostly austere architectural framework with moments of exuberance. The facade has three simple but majestic arched windows, with a series of small windows above and a Star of David in the center. Inside, at the entry to the sanctuary, are golden-hued doors with intricate fretwork. A dome with mosaic detail rises above the engraved wooden ark, which has a golden ornately detailed panel in front. Behind the ark are engraved wooden panels.

B'nai Jeshurun

257 West 88th Street

The Second-Oldest Jewish
Congregation in New York

INDEPENDENT JUDAISM
BUILT 1917–18

In 1825, John Quincy Adams was president of the United States, the Erie Canal opened, and a group of Jews who had been worshipping at Shearith Israel, the only synagogue in New York City at the time, seceded from Shearith to form their own congregation. Founded by Portuguese Jews, Shearith followed Sephardic Jewish ritual, but given there was nowhere else to go, the newer immigrants, Ashkenazic Jews from Germany and Poland, attended services there. Soon they grew weary of following Sephardic rituals and proposed to Shearith that they conduct separate services. They were refused and thus broke off to form B'nai Jeshurun.

Two years later, in 1827, the group found space at 119 Elm Street in what was the First Colored Presbyterian Church and reconsecrated it. As the congregation grew, it moved several times: to Greene Street, West 34th Street, Madison Avenue at 65th Street, and, finally, its current home at 257 West 88th Street.

To design the 88th Street temple, the congregation plucked two architects who were members of the synagogue: Walter S. Schneider and Henry Beaumont Herts, best known for designing the Brooklyn Academy of Arts. They purposefully built the synagogue in what they called "a Semitic character," to prove that synagogues need not be "servile copies of Mohammedan mosques or ape the prevalent styles of Christian churches or Pagan temples." They studied fragments of early Jewish structures to incorporate authentic elements. Ground was broken in 1917 and construction completed in 1918 with the end result being a magnificent building that combines Moorish and Coptic elements.

The interior was designed by Emil Phillipson with a rectangular shape and a gallery on three sides that Robert A. M. Stern's *New York 1900* describes as "a free interpretation of Coptic design, with suggestions from Moorish and Persian sources . . . ensuring a Semitic character that certainly no classic treatment of

190

RIGHT
The floor-to-ceiling
stained glass
windows to the
left of the bimah

OPPOSITE ABOVE
Throughout
the temple are
elaborately detailed
panels and stained
glass windows

OPPOSITE BELOW
Detail of a wall panel

columns and cornices could approach." Throughout the space, mosaics, stenciling, and tiles compose a refined opulence.

The original ceiling was studded with muqarnas, stalactite-like architectural ornamentation that Grove Art Online defines as a "three-dimensional decorative device used widely in Islamic architecture, in which tiers of individual elements, including niche-like cells, brackets, and pendants, are projected over those below." The ceiling collapsed in 1991 and was replaced with a backlit ceiling that creates the ambience of a nighttime sky.

At the entry to the synagogue is a soaring arch within which a rose window displays a Star of David. The copper parapet is echoed by the two towers on either side, which are also copper-clad.

Advent Lutheran Church

2504 Broadway

Graced by Tiffany

LUTHERAN
BUILT 1900–1901

This double-height brick and stone church that sits at 2504 Broadway on New York's Upper West Side is still used by the congregation that founded it 125 years ago. The pitched slate roof protects the magnificent stained glass in both the nave and clerestory designed by Louis Comfort Tiffany and manufactured by his studio. It also protects the other Tiffany adornments, including the ceramic mosaic behind the altar and the sanctuary lamps. The front pipes of the organ are also, untypically, decorated by Tiffany. The stained glass windows depict St. Paul preaching at Athens and Christ returning in glory with angels, the breaking swords beneath them signifying a period of peace.

The Gothic Revival structure was designed by architect William A. Potter, who adopted a German Gothic as opposed to an English Gothic approach, emphasizing the height over the length. Potter was the architect for many of the buildings on Princeton University's campus, including the Chancellor Green Library, Stuart Hall, and Alexander Hall.

In 2000, the Broadway United Church of Christ, which couldn't seem to find a comfortable home and had moved frequently, joined the Advent Lutheran Church after its own Broadway Tabernacle was sold and demolished.

PEACE · GOODWILL
TO · ALL · PEOPLE
WE · PRAISE · THEE

Holy Name of Jesus

207 West 96th Street

From Country Church to City Church

ROMAN CATHOLIC
BUILT 1891–1900

New York City and the rest of the country were still adjusting to a post–Civil War world when Holy Name of Jesus Church came into being in a northwest pocket of the city that was, at the time, a tree-lined suburb called Bloomingdale. In 1868, Father Richard Brennan traveled uptown in a rented buggy with a letter from Archbishop McCloskey in his pocket. In the letter the archbishop introduced Brennan to the Bloomingdale Roman Catholic Association and informed them that he was to be their next pastor.

When Brennan arrived, a small wooden church was already in the process of being built, and a few months later the church was dedicated. A little more than two decades later, in 1891, the work on a new, far more extravagant church was begun. Thomas Henry Poole designed the Gothic Revival church built entirely from Milford pink granite with ornately carved entrances and towers.

The hallmark of the architecture is found in its beam and hammer ceiling executed with highly polished American oak. The lighter colored columns supporting the ceiling contrast beautifully with the darker ceiling. Five intricately carved marble altars grace the sanctuary, with the front panel of the main altar displaying a carved rendition of Leonardo da Vinci's masterpiece, *The Last Supper*. Stained glass windows throughout the sanctuary represent various saints and biblical scenes and figures.

After World War II, there was a great influx of Spanish-speaking Catholics who settled in the area, and the church emerged as a pioneer in its efforts to minister to the religious and social needs of this new community. By the early 1950s, upheaval was wrought by the removal of many residents—who were congregants of the Holy Name of Jesus—from the area to make way for a development project. Most were unable to resettle in the neighborhood and the church lost a great many

parishioners. A similar event happened in 1962 with the initiation of the West Side Urban Renewal Plan, which once again caused many congregants to be displaced and lost to the church forever. Overcoming these setbacks, the church continues to serve the religious and social needs of its community and conducts services in both English and Spanish.

Ansche Chesed

251 West 100th Street

From a Schism to a Synagogue

CONSERVATIVE JUDAISM
CORNERSTONE LAID 1927

An old Jewish joke is told like this: A religious man was shipwrecked on a desert island. When rescuers finally arrived, they saw three huts and asked the man what the huts were used for. One was his home, he explained. Pointing to the second hut, he said, "This is the synagogue I go to."

"And what is the third hut for?" his rescuers asked.

"That?" he responded with a glance toward it. "That synagogue is the one I wouldn't step foot in."

The humor reflects the Jewish disposition for arguing, discussing, disagreeing, ad infinitum. And yes, there is truth in jest, as seen in the many groups of Jews who seceded from one synagogue to form another. Shearith begat B'nai Jeshurun which begat Ansche Chesed, which was established in 1829 when a group of German, Dutch, and Polish Jews seceded from B'nai Jeshurun for reasons unknown.

The congregation first gathered in a rented space on Grand Street, later moving into a building they built for themselves on Norfolk Street, which is now home to the Angel Orensanz Foundation. Several moves followed, migrating northward, as did the population. From 1907 to 1909, the congregation, which was now predominantly German Jews, built a pillared, neoclassical building at the corner of 114th Street and Seventh Avenue (now Adam Clayton Powell Jr. Boulevard) designed by the architect Edward I. Shire. In 1927, it was sold and became the Church of Our Lady of the Miraculous Medal and is now Mount Neboh Baptist Church. Dunlap notes that with the exception of St. Ann's Armenian Catholic Cathedral, the 114th church may be the only sanctuary in Manhattan that has been shared over time by Jews, Roman Catholics, and Protestants.

Shire was the architect for the next and current home of Ansche Chesed at 251 West 100th Street for which he blended Romanesque and Byzantine styles. When

the cornerstone was laid in 1927, Professor Mordecai M. Kaplan said: "It must be admitted that there are a great many Jews who do not find themselves at home in either the Orthodox or the Reform parties. I say parties advisedly because the Judaism of the future will have no schisms, but within it there will be room for difference of opinion." Opened on May 4, 1928, as a Conservative synagogue, Ansche Chesed serves this group to which Kaplan referred.

The exterior is constructed of buff-colored stone and brick. The facade features a triple-arched entryway above which are three tall arched windows. Inside is a barrel-vaulted sanctuary that can seat 1,300 people, who face the highly decorated arch that highlights the bimah and ark. Vibrant decor embellishes the face of the balcony and other interior surfaces. Light filters through beautiful stained glass that fills the numerous windows, door panels, and a three-paneled skylight in the center of the ceiling. In addition to the main sanctuary, the complex includes a six-story community house with classrooms, a gym, a social hall that seats five hundred, a small chapel, and a roof garden.

Just one year after the synagogue opened, the stock market crashed. The ensuing Depression required the congregation to endure difficult years, but it revived as the nation recovered after the Depression. A few decades later in the sixties and seventies, Jews were leaving the Upper West Side and the congregation dwindled precipitously, as did the synagogue's finances. In 1975 the United Synagogue of America, the federation of North American Conservative synagogues, assumed control of the building.

By the end of the seventies, the future was much brighter as the synagogue became a home for the Chavurah movement, in which small groups of Jews with similar sensibilities create autonomous, lay-led minyanim (quorums of ten required for traditional Jewish public worship). The synagogue is host to several minyanim that worship beside the historical congregation, which engages in what is now known as the Sanctuary Service.

Ansche Chesed   205

Church of the Ascension

221 West 107th Street

Brewery Basement to Magnificent Edifice

ROMAN CATHOLIC
BUILT 1896–97

In autumn 1885, New York Archbishop Michael Corrigan decided to create a new parish in the rapidly growing neighborhood of Manhattan Valley that lies north of 96th Street and east of Broadway. One of the neighborhood's earliest landmarks was the Lion Brewery, which was built and run by Catholic Bavarians in 1857 and occupied six city blocks from Central Park West to Amsterdam between 107th and 109th Streets. The basement of the brewery was the home for Sunday mass before the Church of the Ascension was built. Services were also held in the Lion Hall Park Building on 109th Street and then the chapel at the Home for the Aged of the Little Sisters of the Poor on 196th Street. Early attendance was paltry, but by 1896, the congregation had grown to nearly five thousand. The pastor, Father Nicholas Reinhart, eventually found property on which to erect a church. The archdiocese bought eight lots covering an area from Amsterdam to Broadway, from 107th to 108th Streets.

In only a year's time, the church was ready and on Sunday, March 14, 1897, six masses were held. A couple of months later, friends of the Ascension donated a stained glass window that features the Ascension of Jesus. The eleven-by-twenty-two-feet work was made in Munich using a newly developed coloring procedure for glass. This brilliantly hued window still stands atop the main altar.

In 1977, a space that had been the convent of the Sisters of Charity, adjoining the school, was leased to Grace House, part of the Catholic Youth Organization. In March of 1983 or 1984, a treasure of contemporary art was born when Keith Haring set his paintbrush to the stairway walls and created a bold black-and-white mural spanning three floors and eighty-five feet. But after the shelter closed in 2016, the church decided to have it excavated and sold. The cost to excavate was $900,000, but it subsequently sold at auction for $3.86 million in 2019—a record for a Haring mural.

Cathedral of St. John the Divine

1047 Amsterdam Avenue

130 Years Later: Unfinished and Magnificent

EPISCOPAL
CORNERSTONE LAID 1892

The Cathedral of St. John the Divine's cornerstone was laid in 1892, the same year that Ellis Island opened. The great architectural adventure of St. John the Divine began in 1828 when the bishop of New York met with the mayor to discuss the feasibility of building an Episcopal cathedral in New York City. In 1873, the New York State legislature granted a charter for the cathedral, but it wasn't until 1887 that an eleven-acre site was acquired in Morningside Heights. Leading Episcopalian Catholics aspired to build an even grander structure than St. Patrick's Cathedral, so in 1888, the cathedral trustees announced a design contest that drew sixty-eight submissions over a span of three years from top architectural firms, with the winner being Heins & LaFarge. The team presented an eclectic Byzantine-Romanesque style for the majestic cathedral-to-be.

The early years of construction focused on the crypt, and in 1899, the first services were held in the crypt's chapel. The eight massive granite columns that support the east end of the building were transported in 1903 from a quarry in Maine. In 1908, the roof for the Great Choir was completed. In 1909, the master artisan Rafael Guastavino constructed a dome for the crossing with his eponymous tile. Intended to be temporary, the dome still majestically rises above the crossing and remains the largest freestanding dome in the world.

By 1911, the apse, the crossing, and other elements were completed, but the mixed Byzantine-Romanesque style had lost favor with the public. The death of Heins allowed the church to cancel their contract with LaFarge, and in his place they hired Ralph Adams Cram, a champion of Gothic architecture.

During the years of World War I, work progressed and several chapels were completed; however, stoppages were frequent because of the lack of funds. After the war, Franklin Delano Roosevelt headed a building campaign for the cathedral that

208

kicked off in Madison Square Garden in 1925 and became national and international news. Cram built a twelve-foot, one-ton model of the cathedral that was placed in Grand Central Terminal. Gifts poured in from the emperor of Japan, the king of Siam, and Adolph Ochs—the *New York Times* publisher—and thousands showed up for fundraising events, such as poetry readings, boxing tournaments, and horse shows.

John D. Rockefeller generously threw a half million dollars into the till. In exchange, he expected to be appointed a trustee on the board of the cathedral. Claims of welcoming all denominations notwithstanding, Rockefeller, a devout Baptist, was not asked to sit at the table of the board, all of whose members were Episcopalians. His pique impelled him to build his own church to rival St. John the Divine, and the resultant Riverside Church was built speedily with his ample funds.

Despite the rebuff of Rockefeller, the cathedral from the start strove for recognition of all beliefs, if not inclusion. In 1930, Ochs donated two twelve-foot menorahs to thank the bishop, the Right Reverend William Thomas Manning, for his efforts

*The dome of the apse
in a side chapel*

at improving Jewish-Christian relations in New York City. To this day, they flank the high altar.

In 1932, the Great Rose Window, the third-largest in the world, was installed. Forty feet in diameter, it comprises ten thousand pieces of stained glass. It features Jesus surrounded by both Old and New Testament prophets and sixteen angels. Below it is the Lesser Rose Window in the shape of a seven-pointed star.

Four years after FDR's launch, the Wall Street Crash and Great Depression ensued, but the cathedral managed to continue with building. But by the 1930s, living conditions for masses of ordinary people had substantially deteriorated. Bishop Manning led a movement to draw attention to and eliminate the slums and tenements of the city. In 1937, he dismantled an actual tenement and re-erected it at the entrance door of the Cathedral. During this period, on an Easter Sunday, the white congregants of the nearby All Souls church arrived early and locked the doors so Blacks couldn't get in. Bishop Manning "went down there with an axe and knocked the chains off the door."

While the church's involvement in social justice continued, so did construction. By 1939, the first services were
conducted in the nave, and on November 30, 1941, the
entire length of the cathedral was consecrated. A week
later, Pearl Harbor was attacked and all construction
came to an immediate halt. With further building at a
standstill, the cathedral donated five tons of scrap metal
to the war effort.

Under the Very Reverend James Albert Pike, named
the fifth dean in 1952, and Bishop Horace W. B. Donegan,
the pulpit became a forum to tackle current issues and
initiated an era of activity in which luminaries such as
Reverend Dr. Martin Luther King Jr. preached in the cathedral. In 1964, six thousand people crowded the cathedral to support civil rights and end racial discrimination.
In 1969, as part of a nationwide protest, the congregation
engaged in a solemn litany listing the names of all those
killed in Vietnam.

The cathedral also became a center for the literary,
artistic, and intellectual life of the city. Nelson Mandela
and Desmond Tutu have spoken from the pulpit, and
Václav Havel has been honored in the cathedral. Duke Ellington premiered his
Second Sacred Concert in 1968 and Leonard Bernstein performed there on New
Year's Eve, 1983. Concerts remain an ongoing part of the life of the cathedral with
backup from the Great Organ, one of the top ten in the country.

A gilded angel throws a shadow on the stone wall.

Many visual artists from baroque weaving masters to contemporary artists have left
their permanent mark on the cathedral, along with many others' temporary exhibitions. The great bronze doors that depict Old and New Testament stories in bas-relief
panels were cast by Ferdinand Barbedienne of Paris, who also cast the Statue of Liberty.
Elegantly carved fifteenth-century choir stalls separate the narthex from the nave,
while master woodworker George Nakashima's Altar for Peace was crafted from
the trunk of a three-hundred-year-old black walnut tree and dedicated in 1986. And
in 1990, just weeks before he died, the renowned contemporary artist Keith Haring
completed *The Life of Christ*, a bronze and white-gold triptych altarpiece.

One of the aspects of the life of the church, and a favorite among New Yorkers
and people from around the world, is the annual Feast of St. Francis and the Blessing of the Animals. Begun in 1984, the cathedral hosts a service that features a procession of the animals that are welcome inside the church for a blessing in honor
of their patron saint, St. Francis of Assisi. People accompany a vast range of living
creatures, from cats to camels and pups to parrots, all with accompaniment by the
Paul Winter Consort and the cathedral choir performing.

Today, more than 130 years after construction began, the vital life of this mono-
lithic cathedral goes on—as does the construction. In 2017, a structure for the pea-
cocks that have long been in residence in the cathedral garden was built, along
with a new entryway, plaza, and roof over the north transept. Ongoing work to
strengthen and preserve the dome and other areas of the cathedral continues. The
bell tower, designed by Cram and first begun in 1892, remains unfinished.

Upper East Side

Central Presbyterian Church

593 Park Avenue

Good Enough for Rockefeller

PRESBYTERIAN
BUILT 1920–22

In 1821, twenty-two-year-old Reverend William Patton founded Central Presbyterian Church with his wife, Mary, and four others. It began in a schoolroom and then relocated to a church on Broome Street. In 1876, Fifth Avenue Presbyterian (page 126) gave their church, located on East 19th Street, to Central Presbyterian. The parish painstakingly dismantled the Victorian Gothic structure, which was designed by Leopold Eidlitz and built in the 1850s, and moved it piece by piece, rebuilding it at a site they had bought on 57th Street near Seventh Avenue. Later, Central Presbyterian transferred the entire building to 220 West 57th Street. In another unusual transaction, the Madison Avenue Reformed Church at Madison and 57th Street bought Central, and the two swapped homes.

Meanwhile, at 593 Park Avenue, John D. Rockefeller Jr. had commissioned and funded a home for the Park Avenue Baptist Church that was built from 1920 to 1922. It soon proved too small for the congregation, and Rockefeller commissioned the larger Riverside Church, creating an opportunity for the Central Presbyterian Church to buy the Park Avenue building. Central held its first service in its new— and current—home on September 22, 1929.

One of the extraordinary features of the original Rockefeller-funded structure was a bell tower that housed the largest carillon in the world, a fifty-three-bell instrument—even King George V and Queen Mary visited the foundry in Croydon, England, to inspect the bells firsthand before they made their voyage across the Atlantic. Alas, Rockefeller giveth and Rockefeller taketh—when the Baptists decamped to Riverside Church, the carillon went with them, and the bell tower stood empty until a new carillon was installed in 2020.

Temple Emanu-El

1 East 65th Street

A Religious Wonder

REFORM JUDAISM
BUILT 1927–29

In a 2017 feature, CNN highlighted eight "religious wonders" to see in the United States. New York is home to two of them, the magnificent St. Patrick's Cathedral and the equally magnificent Temple Emanu-El. In an article in the *Aesthete* about New York's "most glorious places of worship," Ian Volner said: "Emanu-El's designers broke the mold altogether by making up a new kind of style—part medieval treasure house, part futurist Emerald City—that declares simply and strongly that the Jewish faith merits a place on the wealthiest avenue of the world's most powerful city."

In *American Synagogues*, Samuel Gruber writes that it is "one of the last and largest full expressions of architectural optimism and opulence in American synagogue building before the Depression and World War II." Hyman Grinstein in *The Rise of the Jewish Community in New York 1654–1860* says that "the rise of Emanu-El is one of the most extraordinary in the history of New York congregations. Founded as late as 1845, it rose within ten years to great heights of influence and power." It has continued to attract prominent New Yorkers, including two mayors: Michael Bloomberg and the late Ed Koch.

This impressive congregation was born in 1845 in a rented second-floor space at Grand and Clinton Streets, when thirty-three German Jews gathered to worship. It grew steadily and moved several times to accommodate its growth. In 1847 it moved into a larger space in a former Methodist church and commissioned Leopold Eidlitz to remodel it. He added Stars of David and disguised the round arched windows. From there, they moved to 12th Street, and by 1868, the congregation was prosperous enough to build a Moorish temple designed by Eidlitz and Henry Fernbach. A critic at the time called it "the finest example of Moorish architecture in the world" and the *New York Times* deemed it an "architectural sensation."

By the 1920s, the area around 43rd Street sprouted numerous skyscrapers as it became more and more commercial. At the same time, in 1927, Temple Emanu-El merged with Temple Beth-El, and the joint congregation decided to move uptown. They purchased property at 65th Street and Fifth Avenue, the former site of John Jacob Astor's mansion and ten blocks north of St. Patrick's Cathedral. Jewish architects Robert B. Kohn, Charles Butler, and Clarence S. Stein were commissioned to build the temple, which beautifully blends elements of Moorish, Romanesque, Byzantine, and art deco styles. The architects described the edifice as "Romanesque as used in the south of Italy under the influence of the Moorish, because it was an expression of Occidental and Oriental thought." Architect and critic Kenneth Murchison reported that the new temple left its beholders "speechless at the beauty and majesty of its structure." Construction was completed in 1929 and the temple was dedicated on January 10, 1930.

For the second time, Emanu-El made noise with its architectural prowess, but it had been making another kind of noise within the halls of Jewish thought, as it was at the vanguard of the Reform Judaism movement, gradually shedding some of the practices of the Orthodox forebears. In the earlier years of the congregation, only Hebrew was spoken, which was subsequently replaced with German, and in 1873, it hired its first permanent English-speaking rabbi. At the 43rd Street temple, in 1849, a magnificent organ was installed and instrumental music, heretofore banned, became part of worship services. Other changes from Orthodox tradition included ending the practice of calling congregants to the bimah to read from the Torah, leaving it to the rabbi (except for bar and bat mitzvahs and other special occasions). The most controversial change in the Reform movement was eliminating the *mechitza*, the barrier that separates men and women in Orthodox temples, and thus allowing both sexes to sit side by side and worship together. Temple Emanu-El is considered the flagship temple for Reform Judaism in the United States.

The largest Jewish temple in the world, its sanctuary stands 175 feet long, 100 feet wide, and 103 feet tall and seats 2,500 people, more capacity than St. Patrick's Cathedral. The structure was built with a steel frame, eliminating the need for pillars, making the sanctuary appear even larger—a giant expanse of unimpeded space

OPPOSITE
The upper part of the ark displays a rainbow of marble pillars.

ABOVE
The family name Ochs is engraved in a marble pulpit; the funeral of Adolph Ochs, former New York Times *publisher, was held in the temple.*

in which decorative architectural detail and embellishments abound. To enter the temple, one passes through two bronzed doors bearing geometric art deco detail, which is echoed in the distinctly art deco foyer. In 1930, Clarence Stein wrote of the finished work: "A building which must be small as compared with the skyscrapers of New York must secure its dignity through simplicity of form and largeness of scale."

In the sanctuary the imposing eight-story tall arches are lined with breathtaking mosaics of glass and marble designed by the visionary artist Hildreth Meière, an under-the-radar early twentieth-century artist who has only recently begun to get the attention she deserves. Judaic symbols are woven in her geometric motifs. "You can't imagine how hard it is," she commented to a friend, "to avoid using a cross shape anywhere."

She used glass mosaic pieces, a surfeit of gold, and influences from Spain, Eastern Europe, and mid-nineteenth-century Berlin in her luminous work. Meière's hand can also be seen in some of the ark that was made to look like an open Torah scroll. As is tradition, the ark is on the eastern wall of the building, so as worshippers look toward it and the bimah, they face east toward Jerusalem.

At the west end, above the entrance, is a wheel window designed by Oliver Smith with twelve teardrop-shaped spokes, symbolizing the twelve Jewish tribes, that emanate from a Star of David at the center. The spokes contain stained glass with patterning that recalls the mosaic floors of synagogues from AD 200 to 600. Above the wheel are seven windows representing the seven branches of a menorah. Elsewhere throughout the sanctuary are more than sixty stained glass windows displaying scenes from the Bible and Jewish iconography.

Within the building, there is a second, smaller space: the Beth-El Chapel, which seats 350. The stained glass window over the ark, taken from the temple at 43rd Street, was designed by Louis Comfort Tiffany, as was a World War I memorial plaque.

Church of St. Vincent Ferrer

869 Lexington Avenue

Beauty Contest Winner

ROMAN CATHOLIC
BUILT 1916–18

OPPOSITE
Were it not for the American flag seen on the left, this magnificent Gothic church might be mistaken for one of the great European cathedrals.

Since its founding in 1867 by the Dominicans (Order of Preachers), the Parish of St. Vincent Ferrer (now merged with St. Catherine of Siena) has lived on Lexington Avenue at 65th Street. In 1870, its first permanent church, reputedly in the style of a "Gothic barn," designed by Patrick C. Keely, was dedicated on this same site. About a decade later, a convent adjoining the church, designed by William Schickel, was built on the corner and still stands today.

This "Gothic barn" served the congregation until 1914, when it was demolished. Presiding over the church then was the Very Reverend E. G. Fitzgerald, who was highly impressed by St. Thomas Church, a tour de force by the architectural firm Cram, Goodhue and Ferguson. After its completion, the partnership dissolved, with the members pursuing independent careers. Fitzgerald commissioned Goodhue to build the new church, making it Bertram Grosvenor Goodhue's first solo commission. It was built from 1916 to 1918.

After the church was completed, a jury of architects was convened to select the fifty most beautiful churches in the United States. St. Thomas was awarded first-place winner, St. Vincent Ferrer second. Nevertheless, Goodhue considered it his finest work. All fifty selections were gathered together in the book *Masterpieces of Architecture in the United States*, published by Charles Scribner's Sons in 1930. About St. Vincent Ferrer it had this to say: "The comparison between this church and that of St. Thomas's on Fifth Avenue will reveal at once a trend away from the archaeological and academic in the direction of the free and inspired. While St. Thomas cannot by any chance be said to be a reproduction, yet its details and general character are reminiscent of much that is beautiful in the past. St. Vincent Ferrer, au contraire, possesses of and in itself a beauty which is reminiscent of no particular building or period, but is the product of a happy marriage of grace and genuineness."

Nos autem gloriari oportet in Cruce Domini nostri Iesu Christi

David W. Dunlap is impressed, too. He says that "an ancient architectural vernacular is swept into the industrial age with pistonlike buttresses, not unlike a great ecclesiastical locomotive."

Throughout his career, Goodhue had collaborated with master sculptor Lee Lawrie and did so for St. Vincent Ferrer. Lawrie produced the Great Rook (a large crucifix) on the exterior over the main entrance. It was highly unusual to have a cross affixed to the outside of a church, and it is believed that Lawrie's may be the first on a Catholic church in New York.

The stained glass of the Great Rose Window at the west end of the nave is composed of richly saturated colors with intricate stone tracery. Other stained glass windows display brilliant blues. Deep amber cathedral glass in bold geometric patterns make up the windows without stained glass and are limned with heavy leading.

Dividing the chapels from the south aisle are wrought iron screens that look straight out of one of Europe's finest medieval cathedrals. The pièce de résistance of the interior is Lawrie's exquisite sculpture of the Madonna and Child that is in front of the south chancel pier.

Park East Synagogue

163 East 67th Street

"A Wild, Vigorous Extravaganza"

MODERN ORTHODOX JUDAISM
BUILT 1889–90

OPPOSITE
The magnificent sanctuary
seen from the ladies' gallery

When Park East was built from 1889 to 1890, the architects Schneider and Herter took a no-holds-barred approach to the elaborate Byzantine-Moorish design of the synagogue. The American Institute of Architects (AIA) calls it "a confection that might have been conceived in a Moorish trip on LSD: a wild, vigorous extravaganza." Dunlap calls it "astonishing, almost hallucinatory," adding that "there are few flights of architectural fancy on this scale in New York."

Originally named Congregation Zichron Ephraim, its wondrous design may stem from the fact that it was built with funds from Jonas and Samuel Ephraim as a memorial to their father, Zichron Ephraim. As the single source of financing, Jonas and Samuel likely avoided the bickering and delays to which projects with multiple sources of funding are subject. The brothers, according to Park East's website, "engaged European artists to build an architectural monument of beauty and distinction."

A series of arches of varying sizes create an elaborate portico. Two towers of different heights flank a rose window over the entrance and are replete with multiple cupolas, also asymmetric in their placement. Inside, the luminous beauty of the stained glass rose window, called the "Sun," speaks to the pink, blue, and silver stained glass on the opposite wall over the ark.

The design of the synagogue is anything but subtle and so, too, its spiritual leader for more than fifty years, Rabbi Arthur Schneier, who is outspoken in his advocacy of religious freedom, human rights, and mutual respect. He acts as much a statesman as he does a rabbi. In 2008, when Pope Benedict XVI visited the United States, Rabbi Schneier invited him to Park East, and the pope agreed, making it the first-ever visit by a pope to a synagogue in the country, and only the third papal visit in history to a synagogue anywhere.

230

Seven years later, in April of 2015, Cardinal Timothy M. Dolan conferred a papal knighthood on Rabbi Schneier, citing "'the good works that he's done' to promote religious freedom and international peace," the *New York Times* reported. Papal knighthoods are rarely granted and even more unusual to be bestowed on a non-Catholic.

In the sixties, the Soviet Union's delegation moved into space across the street from Park East, and later there was a bit of a brouhaha when a plaque was installed at the synagogue that read "Hear the Cry of the Oppressed—the Jewish community of the Soviet Union." At the installation ceremony were Robert F. Kennedy and Adlai Stevenson. Their Soviet neighbors were not pleased.

Other well-known names have been associated with Park East. The funeral for former New York mayor Abe Beame was here. And Harry Houdini was in the synagogue's first Talmud Torah class.

Park East Synagogue

233

St. John the Martyr

250 East 72nd Street

Good Things Come in Small Packages

ROMAN CATHOLIC
BUILT 1887 (DEMOLISHED 2020)

OPPOSITE
The interior of the simple,
country-like, Romanesque-
influenced church

The jackhammers, underground blasting, and ugly orange and white plastic barricades that were omnipresent during the construction of the Second Avenue subway didn't diminish the spirit and the mission of this parish founded in 1902, but it couldn't survive the 2014 widespread decommissioning of churches in New York by the archdiocese. The small but impressive Romanesque church that stood at 252 East 72nd Street closed for good in 2015 and was later demolished.

The Romanesque edifice that was built in 1887, originally for the Knox Presbyterian Church, opened its doors in 1903 to the Roman Catholic Bohemian congregation who had purchased it. It had the distinction of being designed by the architect R. H. Robertson, who had initially planned a much larger church with a soaring tower, but those plans were never realized. Only the chapel was erected.

Robertson was a much sought-after architect who built several important churches and buildings in New York and elsewhere in the decades surrounding the turn of the century. Among them were the Academy of Science and Medicine, the Corn Exchange Bank, All Souls church, and the Park Row Building, once the world's tallest office building. His trademark was the application of heavy, rocky-looking brownstone and, while modest in scale, the chapel of St. John the Martyr was a fine example of his work.

Madison Avenue Presbyterian Church

921 Madison Avenue

Fit for a King

PRESBYTERIAN
BUILT 1916

A large suspended cross centered above the altar and between the organ pipes is the focal point of this arts-and-crafts-style church.

The parish of the Madison Avenue Presbyterian Church that stands today at Madison and 73rd Street took a six-decade-long and winding road to arrive here. The church was originally organized as the Manhattan Island Church in 1834 and moved to Fourth Street near the Lower East Side shipyards. It was dedicated in 1842 and known as the Church in the Swamp. (Not to be confused with the Swamp Church on Frankfort Street, nor the Madison Square Presbyterian Church, to which it is not connected.)

It's come a long way from swampland. David W. Dunlap describes the tower of the Gothic structure as one "almost out of King Ludwig's Neuschwanstein Castle." It is crowned with rounded pinnacles and a cone-shaped steeple. With its trio of large arched windows facing 73rd Street, and its steeply pitched roof, it stands out in its staid surroundings.

Around 1839, Manhattan Island Church merged with the Memorial Presbyterian Church that formerly had been the Eleventh Presbyterian Church. Memorial built a Gothic-style sanctuary at 506 Madison Avenue, designed by D. & J. Jardine, and from this point on was known as Madison Avenue Presbyterian Church, but it wasn't yet at its current 73rd Street location. That space was occupied by the Fifteenth Street Church that later renamed itself Phillips Presbyterian in honor of William Wirt Phillips, a venerated leader of Presbyterianism.

The Phillips congregation was housed in a Victorian Gothic sanctuary designed by R. H. Robertson and built in 1873, part of which—the annex that houses meeting rooms, offices, and space for choir rehearsals—still stands. The land had been donated by James Lenox, a well-heeled and well-respected leader among Presbyterians. The area came to be—and still is—known as Lenox Hill. The sanctuary we see today was designed by James E. Ware & Son and built in 1916.

The interior of the sanctuary featured a raked floor with galleries on three sides and is still illuminated by the three divided windows and dormers on the south side and a large window over the west gallery. The facade was altered in the 1960s by the architectural firm Adams & Woodbridge, who replaced three arched doorways adorned with finials with a single carved portal. Other renovations have taken place since then with some new upgrades, such as a new marble floor, but many architectural and decorative features were uncovered and restored. One such discovery in 1998 was oak triforium screens that had been hidden by plywood panels; they were restored to their original splendor.

*The entryway to the balcony
reveals an elegant stained glass
window in the clerestory.*

ABOVE
*View from the gracefully curved balcony,
revealing details of the timber roof*

RIGHT
Detail of a stained glass window

239

Church of the Resurrection

119 East 74th Street

Rustic Charm in the City

EPISCOPAL
CORNERSTONE LAID 1868

As passersby walk along Park Avenue and turn onto 74th Street, the red doors of the Church of the Resurrection immediately beckon to them. The church looks charmingly out of place, like stumbling across a gingerbread house in a concrete jungle. Even among the stately prewar buildings that line Park Avenue, this Gothic A-shaped church seems of a different time and place.

And it is. It is the oldest church on the Upper East Side, originally organized as the Church of the Holy Sepulchre. It was designed by James Renwick Jr., but it is not close to the scale and grandeur of the many other soaring churches he designed, such as Grace Church and St. Patrick's Cathedral, which the well-heeled helped fund.

The Church of the Resurrection was built just east of Park Avenue, on the other side of the tracks so to speak, where those who served the socialites and titans a few blocks west lived. Built as a free church, meaning that members did not have to pay rent for the pews, it was originally known as "the servants' church."

The church, even with its sophisticated stone facade and Romanesque windows, still resembles a country church. The cornerstone was laid in 1868 and the building completed in 1869. In 1991, a major renovation was done during which new stained glass was added and old stained glass uncovered.

Archdiocesan Cathedral of the Holy Trinity

337 East 74th Street

The Seat of the Greek Orthodox
Archdiocese in America

GREEK ORTHODOX
BUILT 1931–32

Bookended by skyscrapers, the church that stands on 74th Street is the seat of the Greek Orthodox Archdiocese of America and the largest of the Orthodox Archdiocese in the Western Hemisphere. The grandeur of the Byzantine Revival cathedral, with its multitude of arched stained glass windows, rose from humble beginnings. The Greek Orthodox parish, the first in New York City, was chartered in 1892 and rented space in what was formerly the Church of St. Benedict Moor. It then moved to the former St. James Church on East 72nd Street, which then burned to the ground in 1927. The congregation was compelled to worship at St. Eleftherios Greek Orthodox Church until its own home was built.

The architectural firm of Thompson, Holmes and Converse, the same team that designed the building that was home to the infamous Tammany Hall gang, was commissioned in 1931, and the building was completed in 1932. Presiding over the laying of the cornerstone was Eleanor Roosevelt, representing her husband, Franklin D. Roosevelt, who was governor of New York State at the time. In 1962 it was designated as the seat of the Orthodox Archdiocesan of America. From 1959 to 1996 Archbishop Iakovos presided over the church and was the primate for the Greek Orthodox Archdiocese of North and South America. Shortly after he was named archbishop, Iakovos met with Pope John XXIII, becoming the first Orthodox leader to meet with a pope in 350 years. Upon his death, the *New York Times* called Iakovos "a towering figure in the ecumenical movement, moving the Greek Orthodox church into the mainstream of religious and political life."

The cathedral is home to a relic of its patron saint, St. Nicholas, which connects the Greek Orthodox—who date back to the time of the consolidation of Christianity in the Roman Empire—with the Dutch who settled New Amsterdam a couple of

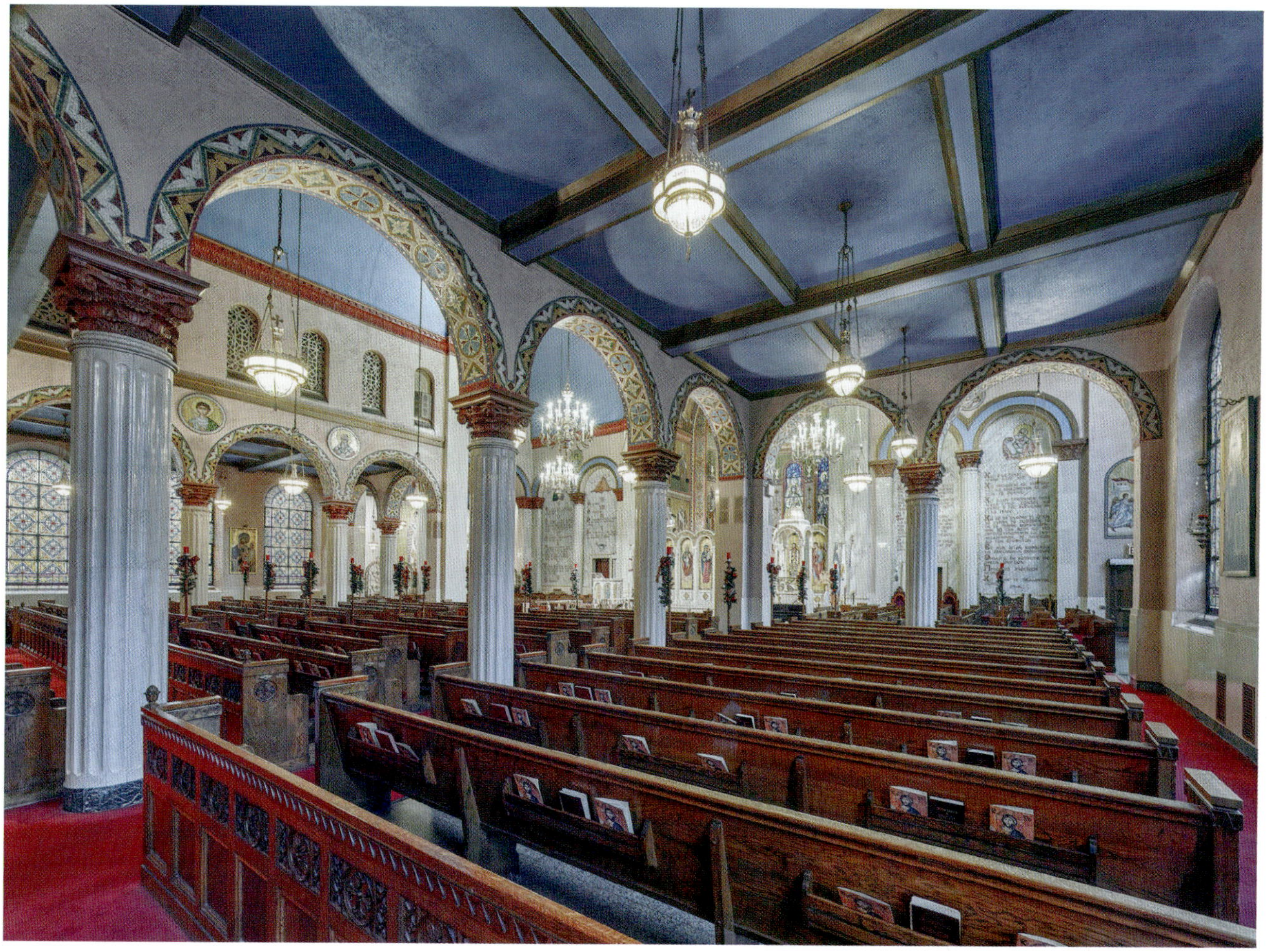

millennia later. The Dutch, too, venerated St. Nicholas as their saint, bridging two very different histories in typical New York fashion.

Characteristic of Byzantine design, the interior is rife with mosaics that line the arches of the colonnades separating the aisles from the nave. The gilded arched panels of the chancel are decorated with paintings, and an elaborately painted dome rises above the gilded apse, beneath which are six arched stained glass windows.

OPPOSITE
The marble chair of the bishop, adorned with mosaics

ABOVE
The arch interiors feature intricate mosaics.

RIGHT
The domed ceiling

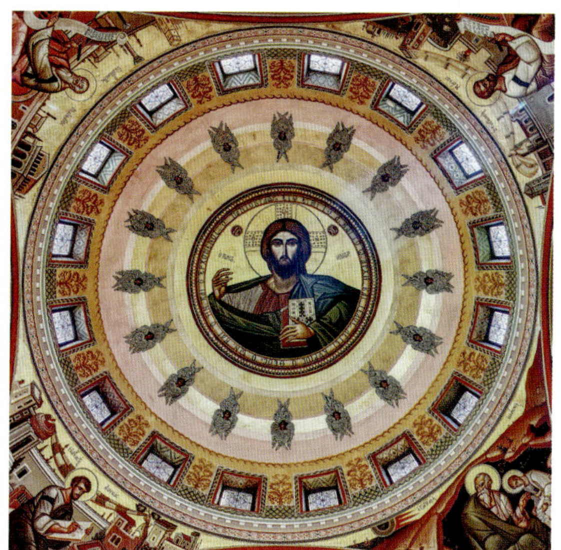

St. Jean Baptiste Church

184 East 76th Street

From a Stable to Splendor

ROMAN CATHOLIC
BUILT 1911–13

Among the waves of immigrants flooding neighborhoods all over Manhattan in the nineteenth century were a group from just north of our border, French Canadians, who made their way to the Yorkville area of the Upper East Side. One of them was Mr. Gabriel Franchère, who hailed from Montreal and was employed by John Jacob Astor's Pacific Fur Company as a secretary. He reported: "In 1810 there were in New York City thirty-two churches, two of which were Catholic. The population was up to ninety thousand, of whom ten thousand were French-speaking." To serve this population, in 1841, St. Peter's Roman Catholic Church (see page 28) built a mission, St. Vincent de Paul Church on Canal Street, and then in 1867 built another on West 23rd Street following the northward migration. By then many had moved even farther uptown, and transportation to 23rd Street via a horse-drawn trolley or the Harlem Railroad was either too slow or too expensive for people to reasonably travel to the church on 23rd. In 1882, a group of French Canadians addressed the problem by forming L'Église de St. Jean Baptiste.

Their first, most inelegant place of worship, fondly called the "Crib of Bethlehem," was above a stable at 202 East 77th Street, where the sounds and smells of their equine tenants—the beating hoofs, the rattling chains, the odors that no amount of incense could disguise—made serene and solemn services nearly impossible. The cacophonous and malodorous conditions were not tolerated for long. Architect Napoleon LeBrun was commissioned to build a nearby church at 159 East 76th Street, which was completed in 1885. The first mass was held in 1884, before the construction was finished.

It was at this location, now known as "Old St. Jean's," that the church became a shrine to St. Anne with the presentation of a relic from Sainte-Anne-de-Beaupré in Quebec. The relic, a piece of the bone from her arm, was brought to New York by

246

REGEM ADOREMVS DOMINANTEM

Bishop Joseph-Calixte Canac-Marquis from Sainte-Anne d'Apt in France, according to the church's website. Monsignor Marquis had obtained the relic while in Rome with the help of Pope Leo XIII.

By the turn of the century, the small congregation that worshipped in a stable had grown considerably, and by 1910, the sanctuary was often standing room only. On one such day, a congregant, Thomas Fortune Ryan, who was a financier and railway magnate, was forced to stand and church lore says that following the service, he approached Reverend Arthur Letellier and inquired how much a new building would cost. Letellier responded, "$300,000." To which Ryan said, "Very well, have your plans made and I will pay for the church." Then, as now, construction projects almost always come in way over budget. In this case, the final bill was approximately $600,000.

Nicholas Serracino, an Italian architect practicing in New York, was commissioned for the project. His design won first place at the Esposizione Internazionale delle Industrie e del Lavoro (the International Exposition of Industry and Labor) in Turin, Italy, in 1911. He employed an Italian Renaissance style, and indeed one might think they have suddenly been transported to Florence and placed in one of the Medici's splendiferous chapels.

The grand limestone facade has a temple-fronted portico and open twin towers. The dome soars 175 feet tall and the stained glass was created by the Lorin Studio in Chartres, France. Old Testament themes are depicted in the luminescent windows. During the church's first decade, the interior was left mostly unadorned, but by the early 1920s, it had been greatly embellished. The high altar is nearly fifty feet in height and composed of Italian marble and mosaic that is flanked by two life-size marble statues. The north and south walls of the church display the fourteen stations of the cross, crafted of mosaics and framed in marble. The boxy pews are "masterpieces of varnished oak," wrote the *New York Times*.

OPPOSITE
This view of the entrance and organ loft shows details of the highly decorated barrel-vaulted ceiling.

ABOVE
The marble altar stands fifty feet high.

Church of St. Monica

413 East 79th Street

Fabergé Elegance and Beauty

ROMAN CATHOLIC
CORNERSTONE LAID 1905

If Fabergé had made churches instead of jeweled eggs for the Russian imperial family, they would look like St. Monica Roman Catholic Church that stands on East 79th Street, whose cornerstone was laid in 1905. The church was dedicated on Thanksgiving Day in 1907, and the following day the *New York Times* had this to say about it:

> St. Monica is one of the largest and finest in the diocese. The interior decorations are especially beautiful. The main altar is forty feet high and is made of the purest Carrara marble, as are also the side altars and statues. The pulpit, altar rail, the altar steps are also of Carrara marble. The Stations of the Cross, the stained glass windows, the quartered oak pews, and the great organ are all on a scale befitting the dimensions of the edifice. The building has a frontage of 80 feet and a depth of 150 feet, and ranks among the largest Catholic churches in the city.

The year the church was opened saw the invention of the gasoline carriage and the electric railway. The Gilded Age, and the extravagance of its titans such as Gould, Vanderbilt, Astor, and Morgan, was raging. While the church itself exudes elegance and architectural sophistication, its congregation was not the posh crowd. It served the masses of Irish immigrants who were flooding into the city and found their way to the Yorkville neighborhood on the Upper East Side.

At the time it was built, there were only three parishes serving the Catholics of the Upper East Side: St. John the Evangelist at 55th Street and First Avenue, St. Lawrence O'Toole (now St. Ignatius Loyola; see page 256), and St. Paul. Father John Treanor felt that these three were not sufficient to serve the growing Catholic

population in the area and petitioned John Cardinal McCloskey, then the archbishop of New York, for permission to create a new parish church. After several months, the archbishop granted the permission to proceed with a new church and the parish of St. Monica was born.

The architectural firm of Schickel & Ditmars designed the church with inspiration from a fifteenth-century French Gothic church in Rouen. One hallmark of this style dating back to the twelfth century is enormous stained glass windows, of which St. Monica has a massive central one that dominates the entrance. The sides of the church are lined with rows of stained glass windows on both the ground level and clerestory. Unfortunately, the buildings that now flank the church make them almost impossible to see from the outside and therefore minimize the illumination they provided years ago. The four stone spires sprouting Gothic crockets are another example of the nearly perfect Gothic touches in the church.

The interior is breathtaking. In between the beams of the pointed arches of the vaulted ceiling, the cerulean blue paint lends a celestial wonder to the nave. The stained glass windows that surround the church give the sense of a magical glass castle. The Corinthian columns and windows are accented with crimson and teal. Contrasting the colors of the windows and the ceiling, as well as the rows of dark wooden pews, is the Carrara marble altar crafted of pure, luminous white, making it a focal point of the sanctuary.

In 2015, as a consequence of the reorganization of the New York Catholic Diocese, the Church of St. Monica merged with St. Elizabeth of Hungary and St. Stephen of Hungary churches.

St. Stephen of Hungary

414 East 82nd Street

An Important Consecration

ROMAN CATHOLIC
BUILT 1927–28 (CLOSED 2014)

In 1901, Reverend Laszlo Perenyi from Eger, Hungary, arrived in New York, and a parish for the city's Hungarian Roman Catholic community was formed. The congregation bought a Presbyterian chapel on East 14th and consecrated the altar in 1904. Like St. Elizabeth (see page 260), also serving the Hungarian community, St. Stephen saw great numbers of their parish moving to the Yorkville section of the Upper East Side. Construction began in 1927 for a new building on East 82nd Street that Emil J. Szendy designed in a subtle neo-Romanesque style in yellow ocher brick. The church was consecrated the following year on December 2 and named for the first king of Hungary, Szent István.

The consecration was a must-do for the congregation. A flyer announcing the event, according to the NYC chapter of the American Guild of Organists website, contained in Hungarian the following warning: "He who is absent from these ceremonies without reason is not a true Hungarian Catholic." Sufficiently forewarned, approximately ten thousand were present at the consecration presided over by Cardinal Patrick Hayes and attended by the consul general of Hungary and other dignitaries. The not-to-be-missed proceedings were followed by a lavish banquet at the Hotel Astor.

At one time the interior featured paintings by the nineteenth-century Italian artist Constantino Brumidi, who also painted frescoes at the Vatican and on the walls, the ceilings, and the interior dome of the US Capitol in Washington, DC. The restored paintings are now in the Church of Our Saviour at 59 Park Avenue.

In 2014 the church merged with Church of St. Monica and St. Elizabeth of Hungary.

Church of St. Ignatius Loyola

980 Park Avenue

A Baroque Masterpiece

ROMAN CATHOLIC
BUILT 1895–98

Of the one and a half million Irish who fled from the devastating potato famine of 1845 to 1849 and immigrated to cities up and down the East Coast, a group of these impoverished immigrants found their way to the Yorkville neighborhood on the Upper East Side. The roots of St. Ignatius Loyola were laid when some of this group gathered together to worship and attend mass in a neighborhood dance hall in 1851. In 1854, they pooled their scarce resources and built a simple wooden structure, the Church of St. Lawrence O'Toole.

Two years later, a much-expanded congregation embarked on an ambitious plan to construct a grander permanent home in the Romanesque style. They bit off more than they could chew. The new building was never completed and nearly bankrupted the congregation, encumbering it with years of debt. Then, in 1866, the administration of the parish was handed over to the Jesuits, who reined in costs, even contributing their own salaries to improve the financial condition of the parish. By 1881 the church was on firm financial footing and again entertained the possibility of constructing a new building. When the ceiling collapsed on a Sunday during mass that year, the desire for a new church became a necessity.

In 1895, on top of the old church, construction began on the limestone facade of a Baroque-inspired building designed by Schickel & Ditmars and dedicated three years later.

When the upper church was completed in 1898, the Jesuits petitioned to have their founder, St. Ignatius Loyola, added as a copatron of the church.

When the NYC Landmarks Preservation Commission officially designated it a landmark in 1969, it had much to say about the splendor of the church:

Monumental in scale and impressive in appearance . . . . The Church of St. Ignatius Loyola is an outstanding example of the Seventeenth Century Italian Renaissance stylistic elements. . . . The facade is well proportioned and beautifully designed, the masonry is of exceptional quality and the carved decoration is outstanding.

Although the Commission judged its eligibility for landmark consideration on exteriors only, the exquisitely rendered Baroque interior would easily meet their rigid standards. Pink granite columns support the sanctuary adorned with marble and mosaics. Stained glass windows "reflect the Jesuit philosophy of honoring God through beauty and permanence," says the church's website.

The church was thriving with more than ten thousand people attending mass on its fiftieth anniversary, according to the *New York Times*. During the ensuing decades, the membership changed as the church attracted social and political members of the beau monde, including the famously Catholic Jacqueline and John Kennedy; Prince Rainier and his wife, Princess Grace, née Kelly, of Monaco; and Mrs. Irving Berlin. The former first lady (later Mrs. Jacqueline Kennedy Onassis) was baptized at the church in 1930 and sixty-four years later, tragically, was eulogized in the same sanctuary. In 2015, luminaries and politicians again filled the pews for the funeral of former governor Mario Cuomo.

Church of St. Ignatius Loyola　　　　259

St. Elizabeth of Hungary

211 East 83rd Street

A Starry Sanctuary

ROMAN CATHOLIC
CORNERSTONE LAID 1891 (CLOSED 2014)

From 1891 to 1892, a Gothic Revival church was built on 345 East 4th Street, between Avenues C and D on the Lower East Side as a place of worship for immigrants from Slovakia, which at that time was still part of the Austro-Hungarian Empire. The cornerstone for this Slovak Roman Catholic parish church, where its first mass was held on April 26, 1891, is inscribed in Slovak.

The fact that the original structure, the first national parish for the Slovak and Hungarian Catholics of New York, still stands today is a testament to the great analogy of New York as a melting pot. While the pastors of St. Elizabeth were purchasing a building from the Lutherans, they sold their building to the Russian Greek Orthodox National Association, which became the Carpathian Russian Orthodox Church of St. Nicholas. It served the emerging Russian immigrant community in the early and mid-twentieth century and displays the royal seal of the Russian czars. Since 1975, the church has housed San Isidoro y San Leandro Western Orthodox Catholic Church of Hispanic Mozarabic Rite, a rarely practiced liturgy outside Spain. (As of 2021, the building was up for sale.)

As the parishioners of the East 4th Street church began heading uptown, following the typical immigrant flow out of the Lower East Side, the pastors and trustees bought a Lutheran church on East 83rd Street, built in 1893. It was designed by Emil Szendy and later altered by Francis Berlenbach. The building still stands, but it has been deconsecrated and closed. The parish merged with St. Stephen of Hungary and St. Monica in 2014.

While the closures of all 140 parishes that were forced to merge in 2014 were heartbreaking, the loss of St. Elizabeth was particularly painful. In 1980, Cardinal Terence Cooke named the Church of St. Elizabeth New York's Roman Catholic parish for the deaf, where worshippers would express in sign language symbols of

260

peace and the words "Jesus," "Lord," "I love you," and more words and phrases of worship. According to the *New York Times*, the church was a haven to nearly five hundred deaf New Yorkers, who not only prayed there but also took classes and socialized. In December of 2021, St. Thomas More on East 89th Street became the new place of worship for the deaf parishioners.

The small size of this jewellike sanctuary was well-suited for the deaf parishioners, as they could easily see the pastor sign mass. The groin vault ceiling is painted in a saturated midnight blue sprinkled with gold stars reflecting the rich colors of mosaics from Ravenna, Italy. Dating back to the fifth and sixth centuries, Ravenna has been a center of mosaic production renowned throughout the world. The exterior of the neo-Gothic church is adorned with a spire.

Church of the Heavenly Rest

1085 Fifth Avenue

Mrs. Carnegie's View

EPISCOPAL
COMPLETED 1929

"I can perceive the heavenly, but where is the rest?" was the comment an observer made about the first home of Church of the Heavenly Rest, founded in 1865 at 551 Fifth Avenue between 45th and 46th Streets, farther south than the present one on Fifth Avenue at 90th Street. Designed by Edward T. Potter, the church had a mere thirty-one and a half feet of street frontage, so he ingeniously treated the front, according to Robert A. M. Stern, as a tower rising not to a spire but to a steep, iron-crested mansard. "Trumpeting angels at the tower's corners, combined with the cresting and the flamboyant tracery of the pointed-arched, west-facing window, conspired to make the building seem at once modern and medieval and distinctly French," described Stern.

The opulent interior held carved polished marble columns and elaborately carved woodwork in the nave arcade and trusses. Comparing it to W. Wheeler Smith's Dutch Reformed church, Montgomery Schuyler, one of the foremost critics of the time, found the design to be "outrageous" in its rage for "unmeasuring novelty." The church won a more favorable view from *The King's Handbook of New York City* (1892), which called it "one of the fashionable shrines of the city."

After a merger with the Church of the Beloved Disciple in 1924 and the change of its neighborhood from residential to commercial, the congregation purchased its current site at 1085 Fifth Avenue. Andrew Carnegie's widow lived across the street in what is now the Cooper Hewitt, Smithsonian Design Museum. The deal came with a caveat: so as not to obstruct Mrs. Carnegie's garden view, the building could be no more than seventy-five feet tall.

Goodhue designed the limestone-clad church but died in 1925, leaving it to his successor firm, Mayers, Murray & Phillip, to complete the project, which they did by Easter 1929. "Their powerful, stripped-Gothic church relied on the striking

contrast of broad areas of bland stonework with large-scale opening filled with delicate Gothic tracery," described Stern. By diluting the Gothic influence, the church evokes modernity. "Its pointed arches echo the energy of skyscraper Manhattan, distinctively informed with an Art Deco aesthetic," reads the church's website.

The sanctuary seats one thousand worshippers, one of whom was New York's legendary mayor Fiorello La Guardia. The vaulted interior is unobstructed by columns, allowing each of the seated one thousand to see every part of the church, including the magnificent altar with its soaring, snow-white reredos. The baptistry is ornamented with enameled mosaics of flowing waters (symbolizing the renewal of life through the power of God's Holy Spirit). The chancel boasts polychrome carvings of Tudor roses and Scottish thistles, while the vaulted ceiling is decorated with stars representing heaven.

In 1993, a fire raged through the church, leaving a path of wreckage, but due to the valiant work of the firefighters on the scene, the stained glass windows were

266   UPPER EAST SIDE

saved. They were able to accomplish this by employing a more complicated—and time-consuming—system to ventilate the one-thousand-degree blaze, according to Dunlap. Scars can still be seen in the two half-melted stone arches in the chancel that have not yet been restored.

The stained glass windows greatly benefit from the low-rise profiles of the buildings surrounding the church, allowing sunlight to stream through. On the north and south sides of the nave, the principal events of Christ's life are depicted. The church entrance is illuminated by stained glass of the west window. Above the reredos is a jewel-toned rose window.

Church of the Heavenly Rest　　　267

Our Lady of Good Counsel

230 East 90th Street

Fairy-tale Beauty

ROMAN CATHOLIC
COMPLETED 1892

Our Lady of Good Counsel, designed by Thomas H. Poole, was completed in 1892, at a time when there was a tremendous migration of people from downtown to uptown. Some moved to get away from the overcrowded and grimy streets of Lower Manhattan, some prospered enough to move to more posh neighborhoods, and some moved for jobs. Yorkville was home to the Ehret and Ruppert breweries, and the Steinway Piano Factory was an easy ferry ride away in Astoria, Queens. When the elevated trains along Second and Third Avenues were completed, Yorkville was no longer remote. Tenements and brownstones were built to accommodate the influx of laborers, and new churches were also established.

St. Lawrence O'Toole (now St. Ignatius Loyola) on East 84th Street, founded in 1851, was overflowing, and Our Lady of Good Counsel was one of many new churches built to meet the needs of the booming Catholic population. Its stately Gothic Revival exterior made of limestone and Manhattan schist has four crenellated turrets, two on either side of the facade, that hint to the baroque castle-in-a-fairy-tale that awaits behind the arched entries.

It is the ceiling that stuns first. Upon the pale blue surface of the ceiling are white designs that are suited for the decoration of a wedding cake or the patterns of delicate lacy fabric. The ten panels of the reredos echo the ornamentation of the ceiling with its intricate patterning and tall finials. The wall behind the reredos has four heavily decorated Gothic arches that frame four paintings of biblical scenes. The tiled floor of the aisles is enhanced with mosaic borders and quatrefoils.

In 2015, Our Lady of Good Counsel merged with St. Thomas More. It is the latter that is considered the parish church, meaning that St. Thomas More is senior to, or overseer of, Our Lady of Good Counsel.

ABOVE
View from the balcony
showing the boxed
pews and chancel

RIGHT
View from the altar
looking toward the organ
and stained glass window

OPPOSITE
The organ loft and
magnificent stained
glass window

Harlem

Salem United Methodist Church

211 West 129th Street

A Harlem Renaissance Gem

METHODIST
BUILT 1887

Salem United Methodist Church began its life in 1881 in a storefront space at 250 St. Nicholas Avenue as a mission of St. Mark's United Methodist Church. From there it moved to a private home until 1908, when the New York City Church Extension and Missionary Society of the Methodist Episcopal Church purchased and renovated brownstones on 133rd Street and Lenox Avenue. This was the same year that Salem officially organized and became the parish it is today.

The founding of Salem United was largely due to the efforts of the Reverend Frederick A. Cullen, a son of slaves who was a Methodist minister and a community and civil rights activist. Coming to New York from Baltimore, he was first assigned to the Lower East Side and then up to the storefront mission in Harlem. He worked with the neighborhood's youth as a way to inspire their parents to become involved in the church and its mission. The success of his endeavors led to the granting of independence for Salem United.

By the early 1920s, the church had outgrown its 133rd Street home with membership at six hundred, and in 1923, the parish bought what had been the Calvary Methodist Episcopal Church on 129th Street. At the turn of the century, the imposing Romanesque structure was thought to be the largest Protestant church auditorium in the city, ministering to the largest Protestant congregation. That status was overtaken when Riverside Church was built by Rockefeller between 1927 and 1930.

Flourishing alongside the great cultural Harlem Renaissance, Salem United became home to prominent members of the arts scene, including opera star Marian Anderson and poet Countee Cullen, the adopted son of the Reverend Cullen. Enhancing the music that is integral to the services here and attracts tourists from around the world is an organ that was originally located in the Waldorf Astoria Hotel. It became part of the church during a renovation from 1949 to 1953.

Salem United Methodist Church

All Saints Church

47 East 129th Street

"The St. Patrick's of Harlem"

ROMAN CATHOLIC
BUILT 1883–86 (CLOSED 2021)

OPPOSITE
The quintessential Gothic style of the ribbed, groined, and vaulted ceiling is also seen in the embellished pointed arches of the ends of the pews.

In 1879, All Saints Church was founded as a Roman Catholic parish. The leaders of the parish had the good taste and good fortune to commission the architectural firm of Renwick, Aspinwall & Russell. It was the great James Renwick, designer of St. Patrick's Cathedral and the Smithsonian Institute's "castle" building, who was the lead designer of the complex, which includes a school and a parish house, that was constructed from 1883 to 1893 and spans the entire block between 129th and 130th Streets on Madison Avenue. The school, completed several years later, was designed by Renwick's nephew, William W. Renwick. In 2007, when the city's Landmarks Preservation Commission officially designated All Saints a landmark, a report said: "Among the many commissions [Renwick] designed during his long career, the Church of All Saints has been called his best." It has long been known as the "St. Patrick's of Harlem."

All Saints is considered Renwick's most fully evolved Italian Gothic Revival style, which was an unusual choice for a late nineteenth-century church in New York, according to New York City's Historic District Council website. "The building displayed the texture, shape, and color variations that were so important during that period due to the writings of John Ruskin." These variations can be seen in the mix of light and dark brick, terra-cotta and stone. The church also has a variety of window shapes, including the uncommon wheel windows of the clerestory. A rose window rises above the entrance. The two spires in the facade are complemented by an elegant bell tower rising from the rear of the church.

Things change quickly in NYC and its churches have had to adapt. The church opened to serve thousands of Irish immigrants who found their way to Harlem. As Harlem's population changed to predominately African American, so did the

parishioners. As the twenty-first century opened, it was home to a large number of Nigerians and even offered a Nigerian mass.

That this magnificent structure served an ever-changing neighborhood of Harlem for more than 125 years is the wonderful story that is New York City. Sadly, in 2015, All Saints was one of several churches in the city that the archdiocese was forced to shutter. Numbers of parishioners had dwindled dramatically to around one hundred; repairs had been neglected for fifty years; pipes burst; the Roosevelt organ, an important relic, hadn't been used in years. In 2019, according to the *Wall Street Journal*, sacred items such as crosses and iconographic stained glass windows—including two by Tiffany—were removed so that the archdiocese could "deconsecrate" the building and sell it. Fortunately, because it is a designated landmark, the exterior cannot be altered.

In March of 2021, the church was sold to real estate developer CSC Coliving, which specializes in shared, low-rent housing. They paid $11 million, a shockingly low price for such a magnificent structure, but still not enough to cover the $13 million of debt that the church had acquired over the years. But then came the good news—Capital Prep Harlem, a charter school with a commitment to social justice, plans to take over the space, giving a second life to this remarkable building and ensuring that the landmark will be preserved.

OPPOSITE
The striking rose window and organ loft

ABOVE
Part of the clerestory and domed transept

Mother African Methodist Episcopal Zion Church

140–148 West 137th Street

"The Freedom Church"

METHODIST
BUILT 1923–25

OPPOSITE
The organ loft and choir
are above the altar, making
music a focal point.

In the latter part of the eighteenth century, John Street Methodist could boast a large Black membership and was outspoken in its firm antislavery stance. However, at services, Black members were relegated to the back of the sanctuary and made to wait until all whites had received communion before they could receive it. In 1796, the Black congregants had had enough of the outrageous discriminatory practices and two of them, James Varick and Peter Williams, left to form the African Methodist Episcopal Church with Varick as its first bishop. It is the first Black church in both New York City and the state.

The founding of AME Zion was not just the establishment of a new parish—it was the founding of a new denomination that combined principles of Wesleyan Methodism and Episcopalian practice supervised by bishops in the Episcopal fashion. Today the more than 1.4 million members of the AME Zion denomination can trace their religious roots to Varick, who conducted the first services in a rented house on Cross Street between Orange and Mulberry Streets. It prospered quickly and in 1800 had sufficient funds to build a modest thirty-five by forty-five wooden church at the corner of Church and Leonard Streets. By 1819 the congregation built a larger stone edifice over the wooden structure.

In 1822, a branch of AME Zion sprouted in Harlem, followed by many more over the years, prompting people to call the original congregation "Mother" Zion. In 1824, Varick's founding church was officially named Mother AME Zion Church. It was here that Sojourner Truth became a member in 1829 when she still used her given name Isabella Baumfree; and it was here in 1843 where she officially changed her name to Sojourner Truth. She was but one of many prominent historical figures who were among the membership over the centuries, including Frederick Douglass, Harriet Tubman, and Paul Robeson, whose brother, the Reverend Benjamin C.

Robeson, became pastor. Other figures include New York's first Black police officer, Samuel Battle; Madam C. J. Walker, the first Black millionaire and first female millionaire; and Florence Mills, a star of the vaudeville stage.

Around the time that Truth joined Mother AME Zion, it became known as the "Freedom Church" because, wherever it called home, it was a stop on the Underground Railroad. Some of its various homes had secret passageways to hide escaped slaves. The nation's first Black newspaper, *Freedom's Journal*, operated from the basement of the church from May 4, 1827, to May 2, 1828.

The church moved from Lower Manhattan to Bleecker Street in Greenwich Village in 1864, and then to 89th Street, where it built a Romanesque church that was completed in 1904. A decade later the Harlem Renaissance was taking root with many Blacks making Harlem their home, and in 1914 the congregation followed this migration, purchasing a former white Episcopalian church on 136th Street.

In the early 1920s, nearby on 137th Street, there was land for sale that the congregation wanted to purchase, but the owner would not sell to Blacks. A white woman acted as an intermediary, purchasing the site on the church's behalf and, immediately following the sale, transferring the deed to Mother AME Zion.

George W. Foster Jr., one of the first professional Black architects in the country, designed the church. Foster's neo-Gothic structure has an auditorium-style sanctuary that many churches preferred so that congregants sitting in the pews would have unimpeded views of the altar and pulpit. Mother AME Zion adopted this plan for another reason. While theaters and entertainment venues like the Apollo and the Cotton Club featured Black performers, the audiences were predominantly white. Blacks, as its current pastor Malcolm Byrd explained in a conversation on the television program *Perspectives*, were not allowed to be *patrons* of the arts. The

auditorium-style sanctuary was planned as a concert hall as much as a place of worship.

In 1936, Reverend Benjamin C. Robeson succeeded James W. Brown as pastor. During his tenure, Robeson was a crusader for civil rights and central to the recognition of key figures of the Harlem Renaissance, including Langston Hughes, W.E.B. Du Bois, Marian Anderson, and even heavyweight champion Joe Louis, all of whom were frequent visitors to the church. Additionally, Lionel Hampton and Duke Ellington conducted concerts at the church.

The minimally adorned interior has arched rows of dark wood pews that mimic the vaulted wooden ceiling. The edge of the horseshoe-shaped balcony is bordered with patterned gilding. Walls of white pointed arches on both sides of the balcony are supported by white columns whose only ornamentation are the gold Corinthian capitals. Stained glass windows surround the walls of the balcony, and above the triple-arched entry is a huge arched stained glass window composed of smaller, tall, slim arched panels with a diamond geometric pattern. At the center is the Virgin Mary and Baby Jesus.

Abyssinian Baptist Church

132 Odell Clark Place

Religion Meets Social Activism

BAPTIST
CORNERSTONE LAID 1922

Whenever the Abyssinian Baptist Church is mentioned in the news or politics, and it often is, it is always accompanied by superlatives: the famed, the influential, the powerful, the historical. Abyssinian Baptist Church in the heart of Harlem is all these things.

On a Sunday in 1808, a group of twelve women and four men from Abyssinia (now Ethiopia), among them several traders, went to a Baptist church on Gold Street to attend services. They were turned away from the sanctuary and directed to a slave loft. Of this event, Adam Clayton Powell Jr. wrote, "Wealthy, educated world travelers, proud human beings, with a well-defined philosophy of religion that matched that of anyone in that auditorium, they resented this and walked out in protest." This abomination led to the founding of the Abyssinian Church we know today when Reverend Thomas Paul, an African American minister from Boston, helped this group of sixteen, plus eighteen members of First Baptist who joined them in protest, to organize the first African American Baptist church in New York State.

The church bought property at 40 Worth Street and remained there until 1854, when it subsequently moved to Waverly Place and then West 40th Street, following the population migration northward in the city. Membership was already growing when Reverend Adam Clayton Powell Sr. began preaching in a tent next to Marcus Garvey's Liberty Hall in Harlem. Membership exploded and Powell became Abyssinian's pastor in its one-hundredth anniversary year.

At the same time, the Harlem Renaissance was blossoming, leading to further expansion of the congregation. The church bought property on the same street that was home to Marcus Garvey's Liberty Hall and from 1922 to 1923 built the structure that stands today. The Tudor Gothic style structure made of limestone was designed by Charles W. Bolton & Son in an amphitheater style. By the 1930s there

were approximately ten thousand members, making it the world's largest Baptist church. By 1941 there were fourteen thousand members.

In addition to leading the spiritual development and reorganization of the church, Reverend Powell also put forth a "social gospel" that blended activism with spiritual leadership and community service. One of its early efforts in this area was in 1928 when the church purchased a home for the aged. Powell was also a member of the NAACP, which was founded in 1909.

In the 1930s, Adam Clayton Powell Jr., following in his father's shoes, began as an assistant pastor and director of the church's kitchen and relief operations that fed and clothed thousands of the needy during the Great Depression. Powell Jr. became pastor in 1937 and launched his career that combined religion, politics, and activism—a volatile combination that earned him a reputation as a militant Black leader who could be flamboyant and outrageous, with little regard for convention.

Powell Jr. was elected to Congress in 1945 and became chairman of the House Committee on Education and Labor. During his tenure, the committee generated or amended more than sixty laws to benefit minorities and the poor. In 1965, twenty years after Powell's election to Congress and the 175th anniversary year of the church, Dr. Martin Luther King Jr. preached from the pulpit.

After Powell Jr.'s retirement in 1972, Samuel DeWitt Proctor, Th.D, known for his

Situated behind the baptismal font, this stained glass window depicts a dove, a symbol of the Holy Spirit.

"quiet activism," succeeded him and took a much less fiery approach to his mission. During his tenure, the imported European stained glass windows were refurbished and a grand Schantz pipe organ was installed. Against this magnificent backdrop, world-class musicians and orchestras, including the New York Philharmonic, Leontyne Price, Billy Taylor, and André Watts, performed in the church.

The current pastor, Reverend Calvin O. Butts III, took the helm in 1989 and has continued the church's efforts in community development initiatives and the fight against discrimination. He established the nonprofit Abyssinian Development Corporation, which is responsible for over $600 million in housing and commercial development in Harlem, and for the $10 million renovation of the Abyssinian church facade and sanctuary.

Twelve years ago, Abyssinian celebrated its bicentennial anniversary with a year of special events, including musical tributes and exhibitions. Nick Ashford and Valerie Simpson wrote an original song for the occasion; the Schomburg Center for Research in Black Culture commissioned artworks, including music CDs; and Wynton Marsalis's *Abyssinian 200: A Celebration*, written for the Jazz at Lincoln Center Orchestra and the United Voices of Abyssinian choir, was performed at Lincoln Center's Rose Theater and at the church. To mark the occasion, several hundred church members retraced the congregation's journey from Worth Street to 40th Street to 138th Street, a three-to-four-hour walk.

Recently, First Lady Jill Biden and Dr. Anthony Fauci visited a Choose Healthy Life COVID-19 vaccination event at the church. Reverend Butts, cochair of Choose Healthy Life's National Black Clergy Health Leadership Council, hosted the event.

Abyssinian Baptist Church

Church of the Intercession

550 West 155th Street

The Architect's Favorite

In the mid-nineteenth century, the area that is now Washington Heights was the tiny hamlet of Carmansville, a verdant green area overlooking the Hudson that was akin to the Hamptons. Well-to-do New Yorkers built summer estates there where they would go to escape the city's stifling summers. Now it is a vibrant, vastly diverse community, the inspiration for Lin-Manuel Miranda's *In the Heights*, and sometimes referred to as "Little Dominican Republic." But in 1842, it was an idyllic spot for John James Audubon, the famous ornithologist and artist who detested the city, to build his home, and he built his working farm there.

It was also ideal for Trinity Church, based at the other end of Manhattan, to buy land for a cemetery. Interred there are luminaries of the arts and members of the beau monde, including Audubon himself, many Astors, Schermerhorns, and the author of the beloved *'Twas the Night Before Christmas*, Clement Clarke Moore (who helped found St. Peter's Episcopal Church in Chelsea; see page 88). However, no chapel for the living stood in the area. Audubon and his neighbor, John R. Morewood, wanted a convenient place to worship and in 1846 formed their own little parish that first gathered in Morewood's parlor. A year later, the parishioners built a charming Victorian Gothic wood-framed building that was subsequently replaced by a hardier stone building at what is now 158th Street and Broadway.

By the end of the century, the parish was facing financial ruin, and in 1903, Reverend L. H. Schwab, whom the blog *Daytonian in Manhattan* refers to as "its wealthy and prominent pastor," resigned on the dubious claim of ill-health. Facing insolvency, the sheriff took possession of the building and the congregation "was allowed the use of the building only by legal sufferance." And then the right man came around at the right time, Reverend Milo H. Gates, a very popular and reputable pastor who was to become instrumental in the good fortune of the church

that was to come. Later in his career, according to his 1939 obituary in the *New York Times*, "Dr. Gates was the only clergyman in the diocese of New York who was a member of the Joint Commission of the Protestant Episcopal Church on Revision and Enrichment of the Book of Common Prayer."

Five years after he joined the Church of the Intercession, the parish was taken over by Trinity and became a chapel of its parish. Almost immediately the vestry of Trinity embarked on plans for a striking new chapel building. Perhaps the vestry's

Church of the Intercession   293

The tomb of the architect Bertram Grosvenor Goodhue with his reclining figure sculpted by Lee Lawrie. Above Goodhue are Lawrie's carvings of many of Goodhue's buildings.

eager magnanimity was prompted by Gates's popularity—during his tenure Intercession could boast 3,500 communicants, more than any of Trinity's other houses of worship, according to the *New York Times*. A decision was made to place the new church on unused land within the gates of the cemetery at what is now 155th and Broadway, which to some seemed a peculiar choice.

Trinity commissioned the top architectural firm of Cram, Goodhue and Ferguson, renowned for their designs of Gothic Revival buildings. It was Bertram Grosvenor Goodhue, designer of other masterworks including St. Thomas Epis and St. Barts, who would be the sole partner on the project, and he reportedly considered it his crowning work. Widely viewed as one of the most beautiful ecclesiastical structures in the United States, Intercession was built from 1911 to 1914.

The laying of the cornerstone on October 24, 1912, was an event accompanied by "a procession of lay and clerical officials, preceded by the chapel choir and trumpeters," who marched from the old dilapidated church on 158th Street to the new building, reported the *American Scenic and Historic Preservation Society* magazine.

Goodhue built Intercession on a grand scale with a length of two hundred feet, width of seventy feet, and height of eighty-one feet. While Goodhue was managing the overall grand scheme, Gates had some creative thoughts of his own. At the turn of the century, Gates had visited a small mountain church in northern Spain where he saw an altar that incorporated bits of derelict Moorish sculpture and was inspired to make Intercession's altar an artistic reliquary as well. Integrated in the altar are 1,563 bits of stones including pieces from Jericho, Mount Sinai, the Wailing Wall, and even Canterbury Cathedral. The altar is but one of the highlights of the interior. Historian John Renner writes that "exquisite carvings

abound in the building. The roof is supported by massive beams and a wood ham-
mered ceiling that gives the nave a flavor of a baronial banquet hall with colorful
banners."

Gates was a proponent of "cheerful sermons" during which he would disparage
the typical solemn pulpit talks. His effervescence is on display in the Christmas
tradition he initiated, the Clement Clarke Moore Candlelight Carol Service, in 1911.
Each year children sit on the altar steps while Moore's beloved poem is read by special guests. Following the service in which traditional carols are sung, the children,
carrying lanterns, process to the grave of Moore to pay homage. Renner states that
it "has become the oldest and most widely publicized Christmas tradition in northern Manhattan."

Although the sanctuary is gorgeous, it's the crypt that steals the show. Prior to his
death, Goodhue requested that he be buried in the chapel. He felt Intercession was
his best work, although others may disagree, given some of his previous successes
such as the Cathedral of St. John the Divine and the magnificent St. Thomas Church
on Fifth Avenue.

Goodhue could not have imagined the extraordinary memorial that was designed
for him, according to Renner, "in the Protestant interpretations of the royal tombs
of Saint Denis," by the renowned sculptor Lee Lawrie. The reclining carved figure
of Goodhue is surrounded by miniature sculptures of many of his buildings. The
inscription reads: "Bertram Grosvenor Goodhue, 1869–1924. This tomb is an affectionate token of his friends. His great architectural creations that beautify the land
are his monuments." The crypt is believed to be the first columbarium in a church
for the ashes of the parishioners who have been cremated.

*The Gothic crypt echoes
the beauty above.*

Acknowledgments

For my wife, Roselyne, invaluable and intrepid partner on this eight-year odyssey.

To my writer, Elizabeth Anne Hartman, who helped make this book a reality.

To Craig R. Whitney, who has graced us with such a beautiful and heartfelt foreword.

To my dear friends Diana and Sean Cranor, owners of Camera West, who saw to it that I was always able to photograph with the finest equipment.

And not least, to the incredible women and men of Manhattan's religious community, who opened not only their doors, but their hearts.

I am grateful.

For those who are photographically curious, the equipment I used is as follows:

- Alpa Max with the following Rodenstock lenses: 23 mm, 32 mm, 50 mm, 70 mm, 90 mm, 180 mm
- A succession of Phase One digital backs, culminating in the IQ4 150 (150+ megapixels)
- Arca-Swiss geared cube head and a Gitzo carbon fiber tripod

The camera case weighs sixty-five pounds.

—MICHAEL L. HOROWITZ

This book would not have happened if my dear friend Sue hadn't dragged me along on an errand to pick up photographic work from Michael's studio. Her friendship, my sister Vicki's ongoing support of every cockamamie idea I have, my partner Dennis's belief in me, and my son Jake and his wife Tara's cheerleading made this possible. I love you all. And, of course, to Michael, who invited me to join his passion.

Thanks also to Meg Parsont who connected me to David Fabricant who, subsequently, kindly answered my call. And thanks to the rest of the Abbeville team for being such a pleasure to work with and making this book as beautiful as Michael's photographs.

—ELIZABETH ANNE HARTMAN

Recommended Reading

BOOKS

Cook, Leland. *St. Patrick's Cathedral: A Centennial History*. New York: Quick Fox, 1979.

Dunlap, David W. *From Abyssinian to Zion: A Guide to Manhattan's Houses of Worship*. New York: Columbia University Press, 2004.

Dunlap, David W. and Joseph J. Vecchione. *Glory in Gotham: Manhattan's Houses of Worship: A Guide to Their History, Architecture and Legacy*. New York: City and Company, 2001.

Gruber, Samuel D. *American Synagogues: A Century of Architecture and Jewish Community*. New York: Rizzoli, 2003.

Hall, Edward Hagaman. *A Guide to Cathedral Church of Saint John the Divine in New York City*. Scholar Select series edition, Andesite Press, 2017. First published 1921.

Kelly, George A. *The Story of St. Monica's Parish*. New York: Monica Press, 1954.

Smith, Bill and Wayne Pearson. *A Cathedral for the 21st Century: An Oral Biography of the Cathedral of Saint John the Divine*. New York: Saint John the Divine, 2019.

Stern, Robert A. M., Thomas Mellins, and David Fishman. *New York 1880: Architecture and Urbanism in the Gilded Age*. New York: Monacelli Press, 1999.

White, Norval and Elliot Willensky. *AIA Guide to New York City: The Classic Guide to New York's Architecture*. 4th ed. New York: Three Rivers Press, 2000.

Wolfe, Gerard R. *The Synagogues of New York's Lower East Side: A Retrospective and Contemporary View*. 2nd ed. New York: Empire State Editions, 2012.

Wright, Robert J. *St. Thomas Church Fifth Avenue*. Grand Rapids: William B. Eerdmans Publishing Co., 2001.

WEBSITES

Many churches have a wealth of information about their history and architecture on their individual websites.

"The Bialystoker Synagogue—Astrological Paintings." Richard McBee: Artist & Writer. October 29, 2001. https://www.richardmcbee.com/writings/jewish-art-before-1945/item/the-bialystoker-synagogue-astrological-paintings.

CNN Travel. https://www.cnn.com/travel/article/beautiful-religious-sites-us/index.html

The Internet History Sourcebooks Project. Fordham University. https://sourcebooks.fordham.edu/medny/stpat1.asp.

The New York City Chapter of the American Guild of Organists. www.nycago.org.

The New York Landmarks Conservancy. Tourist in Your Own Town series. https://nylandmarks.org/explore-ny.

NYC-ARTS. www.nyc-arts.org.

BLOG

Daytonian in Manhattan. http://daytoninmanhattan.blogspot.com.

Index

Abyssinian Baptist Church,
    9, 181, 286–89
    bicentennial anniversary, 289
Abyssinian Development
    Corporation, 289
"Actors' Church," 102
Adams, Herbert, 150
Advent Lutheran Church, 194–97
African Americans, 278.
    See also Blacks
African Methodist Episcopal
    Zion Church, 23
Ahawath Chesed Shaar
    Hashomayim, 159
Alcoholics Anonymous (AA), 132
Allen Street Methodist
    Episcopal Church, 54
All Saints Church (closed),
    144, 278–81
All Souls church, 214, 234
Americanism, 108
AME Zion denomination, 282
Anderson, Marian, 274, 285
Angel, John, 144
Anglican churches, 14
Anglicanism, 14
Anne, St., 246
Ansche Chesed, 202–5
anti-Catholicism, 58
anti-Catholic laws, 10
antislavery positions, 282
Apollo Theater, 181, 284
Archdiocesan Cathedral of
    the Holy Trinity, 242–45
art deco style, 125, 129,
    153, 223, 225
Astor, Caroline Schermerhorn,
    31
Astor, John Jacob, 16,
    58, 110, 223, 246
Astor, William, 16, 113
Astor, William B., 16
Astor, William Waldorf, 16
Audubon, John James, 290

Bait Ha'Knesset Anshi
    Bialystoker, 46

baldachin, 144, 167, 185
Baptist churches, 178,
    181, 286, 288
Baptists, 218
Barbedienne, Ferdinand, 215
basilica, 83, 164
Basilica of St. Patrick's
    Old Cathedral, 56–61
Bellevue Hospital, 139
bells, 147, 218
    law against, 42
    of Trinity Church, 14
    ringing of, 129
Benedict XVI, Pope, 147, 230
Bennett, James Gordon Jr., 102
Bèrard family, 31
Berlenbach, Francis, 260
Berry, Luke, 42
Beth-El Chapel, of Temple
    Emanu-El, 225
Beth Hamedrash (House
    of Study), 34
Bethune, Joanna, 126
Bialystok, Poland, 46
Bialystoker Synagogue, 46–49
Bishir, Catherine W., 16
Bitter, Karl, 16
Black churches, 282
Blacks
    congregations of, 23
    discrimination against
        in churches, 282
    treatment of, by white houses
        of worship, 11, 86, 181, 214
Blessing of the Animals, 215
Bloomingdale, 198
B'nai Jeshurun, 170,
    171, 190–93, 202
Bohemians, 156
Bonawit, G. Owen, 129
Bowery, 80
breadlines, 98
Brennan, Richard, 198
Brevoort, Henry Jr., 76, 79
Brick Church, 72–75
Broadway United Church
    of Christ, 194

Brophy, Martin J., 116
Brown, James W., 285
Brown, Thomas McKee, 110–11
brownstone, 16, 24
Bruges *Madonna*, 167
Brumidi, Constantino,
    102, 104, 136, 254
Brunner & Tryon, 171
Buchman, Frank Nathan
    Daniel, 132
Burleigh, Henry Thacker, 86
Burns, George, 54
Bush, George H. W., 26
Butler, Charles, 223
Buttons, Red, 54
Butts, Calvin O. III, 289
Byrd, Malcolm, 284
Byzantine architecture, 182
Byzantine-Moorish style, 230
Byzantine Revival, 242
Byzantine-Romanesque
    style, 150, 153, 202, 208
Byzantine style, 106, 223, 242

Calvary Church, 132–35
Calvary Methodist
    Episcopal Church, 274
Canac-Marquis, Joseph-
    Calixte, 249
Cantor, Eddie, 54
Capital Prep Harlem, 281
Capuchin Order, 28, 109
Carcaterra, Lorenzo, 119
Carmansville, 290
Carmelite friars, 136
Carnegie, Andrew, widow of, 264
Carpatho-Russian Orthodox, 68
Cathedral of St. John the
    Divine, 175, 208–15
cathedrals, 58, 229
    importance of, historically, 140
Catholic churches, 28, 32, 40, 42,
    56, 58, 64, 68, 80, 94, 98, 102,
    106, 109, 116, 136, 140, 164, 172,
    182, 198, 206, 226, 229, 234, 246,
    250, 254, 256, 260, 268, 278
Catholic diocesan schools, 31

298

Catholics, 106
    immigrants, 58, 140
    public worship forbidden
        to, 10, 28
cemeteries, 42, 58
Central Presbyterian
    Church, 218–19
Central Synagogue, 156–61
Charles III of Spain, 31
Charles W. Bolton & Son, 286
Chartres Cathedral, 94
Chavurah movement, 205
Chevra Anshei Chesed
    of Białystok, 46
Chinese, 32, 56
choir, 147
Christ Protestant Episcopal
    Church, 32
churches, moving uptown, 20–23,
    76, 120, 186, 246, 260, 268, 286
Church in the Swamp, 236
Church of England, 24, 72, 110
Church of Our Saviour, 254
Church of St. Francis
    of Assisi, 98–101
Church of St. Francis
    Xavier, 80–83
Church of St. Mary the
    Virgin, 94, 110–15
Church of St. Monica, 109, 250–54
Church of St. Paul the
    Apostle, 164–67
Church of St. Vincent
    Ferrer, 226–29
Church of Scotland, 72
Church of St. Lawrence
    O'Toole, 256
Church of St. Nicholas, 260
Church of the Ascension, 206–7
Church of the Beloved
    Disciple, 264
Church of the Blessed
    Sacrament, 172–75
Church of the Heavenly
    Rest, 264–67
Church of the Holy Sepulchre, 240
Church of the Intercession,
    290–95
    Trinity Church takeover
        of, 293–94
Church of the Resurrection,
    123, 240–41
Church of the Sacred Heart
    of Jesus, 116–19
Church of the Transfiguration,
    32–33, 40, 175
Civil War, 23, 45, 143, 159, 178, 198

Clarke, Molly, 88, 90
Clarke, Thomas, 88
Classical architecture, 50
Clayton & Bell, 79
Colapietro, Peter, 109
Collegiate Reformed Protestant
    Dutch Church, 176
Colonial style, 24
columbarium, 295
Congregation Ahawath
    Chesed, 156
Congregation Rodeph
    Sholom, 186–89
Congregation Shaarey
    Shamoyim, 54
Congregation Shearith
    Israel, 168–71, 190, 202
Congregation Zichron
    Ephraim, 230
Conservative Judaism
    synagogues, 202, 205
Considine, Father, 182
Cooke, Terence, 142, 260
Coppo, Ernest, 32
Coptic style, 190
Corridan, John M., 80
Corrigan, Michael, 119, 172, 206
Cotton Club, 284
Cram, Goodhue and Ferguson,
    123–25, 226, 294
Cram, Ralph Adams, 123–24,
    175, 208, 211, 215
Crèvecœur, Hector St. John de,
    28
crypt, 146, 208, 295
CSC Coliving, 281
Cullen, Countee, 274
Cullen, Frederick A., 274

Da Ponte, Lorenzo, 59
Darwinism, 75
Daub, Sidney, 50
day schools, 189
deaf worshippers, 260, 263
decommissioning of churches,
    234
deconsecration of churches, 281
Democratic Party, 116
Depression, 10, 19, 49, 98,
    186, 205, 214, 220, 288
Deson, George, 164
de Valera, Éamon, 136
discrimination, 32, 215, 289
D. & J. Jardine, 236
Dodge, Jeremiah, 178
Dohány Street Synagogue
    (Budapest), 160

Dolan, Timothy, 147, 149, 233
domes, 34, 37, 39, 45, 136, 150,
    153, 167, 178, 185, 189, 208,
    214, 215, 245, 249, 254, 259
Dominicans (immigrants), 56
Dominicans (Order), 226
Donegan, Horace W. B., 215
doors, 16, 46, 49, 135, 144,
    150, 153, 160, 185, 189,
    214–15, 225, 239–40
Douglass, Frederick, 282
draft riots, 45, 108
Dubois, John, 64
Du Bois, W.E.B., 285
Duffy, Francis, 108
Duffy, Patrick, 64
Dunlap, David W., *From
    Abyssinian to Zion: A
    Guide to Manhattan's
    Houses of Worship*, 10
Dutch Colonial style, 176
Dutch Reformed Protestant
    churches, 176
Dutch settlers, 242
Dutch West India Company,
    168
Dvořák, Antonín, 86
Dzubaj, Bishop, 68

ecclesiological movement, 16
Edward VIII, 19
Eidlitz, Leopold, 182, 218, 220
Eldridge Street Museum, 39
Eldridge Street Project, 39
Eldridge Street Synagogue, 34–39
Ellington, Duke, 129, 215, 285
Embury, Philip, 20
Engelbert, Henry, 32, 60
Ephraim, Jonas and Samuel,
    230
Episcopal cathedral, 208
Episcopal churches, 9, 14, 24, 32,
    54, 76, 84, 88, 94, 110, 120, 132,
    150, 208, 240, 262, 274, 290, 293
Episcopalians, 24, 72, 75, 110, 211
    orthodox, 110
Erben, Henry, 58
Erhardt, Henry, 98
Eucharist, schedule of, 110

Farley, John Murphy, 144
Federal style, 46
female congregants, 49, 50
Fernbach, Henry, 159–61, 220
Fifth Avenue Presbyterian
    Church, 126–29, 218
films, 58

fires, 14, 20, 24, 42, 58, 60, 64,
    75, 83, 84, 86, 94, 97, 106, 119,
    120, 123, 124, 156, 160–61, 266
First Baptist Church, 178–81
First Century Christian
    Fellowship, 132
First Presbyterian Church, 72–75
First Roumanian
    American Congregation
    (demolished), 54–55
Fish, Hamilton, 70
Fitzgerald, E. G., 226
Five Points area, 32
Fletcher, Benjamin, 14
Floyd, George, protests (2020), 58
Fordham University, 146
Fosdick, Harry Emerson, 75
Foster, George W. Jr., 284
Franchère, Gabriel, 246
Francis, Pope, 149
Francis of Assisi, St., 215
free chapels, 110, 123, 143, 240
French, Daniel, 150
French Canadians, 246
French Gothic, 94, 110, 113, 253
Frey, Bonaventure, 94
Fulton, Robert, 19
fundraising, 59, 97, 106,
    110, 143, 211

Gallatin, Albert, 19
Gangs of New York (film), 58
Gano, John, 178
Gans, Deborah, 39
gardens, 153, 155, 205, 215, 264
Gardoqui, Diego de, 28, 30–31
Garment Center, 104
Gates, Milo H., 290, 293–94
Gates of Paradise (Florence), 16
Gautier, Andrew, 24
General Theological Seminary, 91
Georgian style, 24, 42
German Catholics, 94
German Gothic, 40, 194
German Jews, 170, 202, 220
German Roman Catholic
    Church of St. John, 94
Ghiberti, Lorenzo, 16
Gibson, Robert W., 176
Gilded Age, 37, 120, 250
The Godfather (film), 58
Goodhue, Bertram Grosvenor,
    124, 125, 150, 153, 155, 164, 167,
    226, 229, 264, 294, 295
Gothic Revival, 16, 60, 91,
    102, 120, 132, 135, 140, 178,
    194, 198, 260, 268, 294

Gothic style, 8, 14, 16, 56, 68, 70,
    72, 79, 94, 104, 116, 120, 123–26,
    144, 149, 164, 167, 172, 182,
    208, 218, 226, 236, 240, 250,
    253, 264, 266, 267, 278, 295
Grace Church, 70, 76–79,
    144, 150, 240
Gramercy Park, 132
Gratz, Roberta Brandes, 39
graveyards, 56–58
Great Fire of 1776, 14, 24
Great Seal of the United
    States of America, 27
Great White Way, 102
Greco-Roman design, 168, 171
Greek Jews, 50
Greek Orthodox Archdiocese
    of America, 242
Greek Orthodox Cathedral, 242
Greek Revival, 20, 31, 42, 64, 91
Gregorian chant, 9, 147
Guastavino, Rafael, 153, 182, 208

Hadas Yeshuan congregation, 46
Haggerty, John R., 31
Hagia Sophia, Istanbul, 182
Hamilton, Alexander, 19, 31
Hampton, Lionel, 285
Haring, Keith, 206, 215
Harkness, Anna Marie, 129
Harlem, 181, 274–95
Harlem Renaissance, 274, 284–86
Harper, James, 23
Hassam, Frederick Childe, 134
Havemeyer, Henry Osborne, 172
Havlish, Fiona, 27
Hayes, Patrick, 254
Hearst, William Randolph, 102
Heaton, Clement J., 175
Heck, Barbara Ruckle, 20
Hecker, Isaac Thomas, 164, 167
Heeney, Cornelius, 58
Heins (architect), 208
Heins & LaFarge, 208
Hell's Kitchen, 80, 106–8, 115, 119
Herald Square, 102, 104
Herter, Gustave and Christian, 37
Herter, Peter and Francis
    William, 37
Herts, Henry Beaumont, 190
Hogan, James Humphries, 125
Holiday, Henry, 79
Holkhe Yosher Vizaner, 34
Holy Cross Church, 97, 106–9
Holy Name of Jesus, 198–201
Holy Trinity Catholic
    Church, 182–85

Huebsch, Adolph, 156
Hughes, John, 32, 64, 106, 140–43
Hughes, Langston, 285
Hungarians, 254, 260
Hunt, Richard M., 16
hurricane of 1938, 39

Iakovos, Archbishop, 242
immigration, 10–11, 34
Independent Judaism
    synagogues, 190
interfaith worship, 27
Ioannina, Greece, 50
Irish, 8, 11, 28, 30, 32, 42,
    45, 56, 58, 106, 116, 136,
    140, 143, 250, 256, 278
Italian Franciscan style, 40
Italian Gothic Revival, 278
Italian Renaissance style, 249
Italians, 11, 32, 40, 56

Jackson, Betsy, 126
James E. Ware & Son, 236
Jardine, D. & J., 236
Jesuits, 256
Jews
    Ashkenazic, 170–71, 190
    immigrants, 45
    public worship forbidden
        to, 8–10, 168
    Sephardic, 168–71
    Spanish and Portuguese,
        10–11, 168
Jogues, Isaac, 28
John Street United Methodist
    Church, 20–23, 282
John XXIII, Pope, 242
Judaism
    Orthodox, 37, 45, 156,
        186, 205, 223
    Reform, 9, 37, 186, 189, 205, 223
Judge, Mychal F., 31, 101

Keble, John, 110
Keely, Patrick C., 42,
    83, 102, 104, 226
Kehila Kedosha Janina Synagogue
    and Museum, 50–53
Keister, George M., 178, 181
Kennedy, John and Jacqueline, 259
Kennedy, Robert F., 147, 149, 233
Khal Adas Jeshurun, 34, 37
Kimbel & Cabus, 128
King, Martin Luther Jr., 215, 288
Kirkland, Bryant M., 129
Kirkland Chapel, 129
Know-Nothings, 10, 42, 58, 140

Knox Presbyterian Church, 234
Koegel, David, 49
Kohn, Robert B., 223
Koppe, Simon, 45
Kosher dietary laws, 49
Kunz, Zachary, 98

La Farge, John, 123, 164, 167, 208
Lamprecht, William, 83
Landmarks Preservation
    Commission, 32, 155,
    160, 164, 256, 278
languages in New York, 30
Larkin, John, 80–83, 105
Lawrie, Lee, 123, 124,
    153, 229, 294, 295
LeBrun, Napoleon, 94,
    113, 116, 246
L'Enfant, Pierre, 27
Lenox, James, 236
Lenox Hill, 236
Leonardo da Vinci, 198
Letellier, Arthur, 249
liberalism (Judaic), 156
Lion Brewery, 206
Little Italy, 40
lobster, picture of, 49
Longacre Square, 102,
    104, 106, 110
Lorin Studio, 249
Louis, Joe, 285
Lower East Side, 34, 39, 40, 46,
    50, 260
Lutheran churches, 194
Lutherans, 14, 260
Lutz, Joseph Anthony, 106

Macy's, 104
Madigan, Father, 31
Madison Avenue Presbyterian
    Church, 236–39
Madison Avenue Reformed
    Church, 218
Madison Square Church, 75
Maginnis, Charles D., 144
Makemie, Francis, 72
Malibran, Maria, 59
Mangin, Joseph-François, 60
Manhattan Island Church, 236
Manhattan Valley, 206
Manning, William
    Thomas, 211, 214
Marani, Philip, 139
Margreiter, Rudolph, 98
Markoe, James Wright, 86
Mark the Evangelist, St., 71
Martiny, Philip, 150

Maryknoll Fathers, 32
Mayers, Murray & Phillip, 264
McBean, Thomas, 24
McCaffrey, Joseph, 108, 109
McCloskey, John, 56, 64, 94,
    98, 116, 143, 146, 198, 253
McFadden, Stephen, 109
McGlynn, Edward, 136
McGuire, Joseph A., 182
McKim, Mead & White,
    75, 102, 176
Mean Streets (film), 58
Medieval Gothic, 164
Megapolensis, Johannes, 176
Meière, Hildreth, 150, 153, 154, 225
Memorial Presbyterian
    Church, 236
Methodism, 20
Methodist churches,
    20, 46, 274, 282
Meyers, Charles B., 186
Mill Street Synagogue, 168, 171
Mingey, Lawrence P., 116–19
modernism (heresy), 108
modern orthodox Judaism, 230
Montgomery, Richard, 27
Montgomery Monument, 27
Moore, Annie, 45
Moore, Benjamin, 88, 91
Moore, Clement Clarke,
    88, 91, 290, 295
Moorish architecture, 50, 116,
    156, 160, 190, 220, 230
Moorish Revival, 160
Moorish style, 37, 39, 220, 223
Morehouse, Clifford P., 16
Morewood, John R., 290
Morgan, J. P., 84–86
mosaics, 16, 83, 98–101, 124,
    150, 153, 154, 167, 185, 189,
    193, 194, 225, 242, 245,
    249, 259, 263, 266, 268
Mother African Methodist
    Episcopal Zion Church, 282–85
Mount Neboh Baptist Church, 202
Mozarabic Rite, 260
murder in churches, 86
music in churches, 9, 59,
    128, 129, 147, 274, 289

Nakashima, George, 215
National Historic
    Landmarks, 8, 39, 155
nativists, 10, 42, 58
Neapolitan Baroque style, 40
Nelan, Kevin J., 119
New Netherland, 70

New York City
    1970s decline of, 97
    colonial, 14
    nation's capital, 28
    primacy among US cities, 16
New York City Fire
    Department, 101, 116
New York City Police
    Department, 108
New York Landmarks
    Conservancy, 24, 39
Nicholas, St. (at Christmas), 242
Nicholas of Myra, St., 68
Nigerians, 281
Nightworkers' Mass, 98
Núñez de Haro, bishop, 31

Ochs, Adolph, 211, 223
O'Connor, Andrew, 150
Old St. Pat's, 56
Onassis, Mrs. Jacqueline
    Kennedy, 259
O'Neill, Eugene, 102
On the Waterfront (film), 80
organs, 58, 147
Orgues Létourneau, 64
O'Rourke, Jeremiah, 164
Orthodox Judaism synagogues,
    34, 46, 54, 168
Our Lady of Altagracia, 56
Our Lady of Good Counsel, 268–71
Our Lady of the Scapular
    (closed), 136–39
Owen, Dale, 79
Oxford Group, 132
Oysher, Moishe, 54

Pacino, Al, 58
Park Avenue Baptist Church, 75,
    218
Park East Synagogue, 230–33
Park Row, 102
Patrick, St., 56
Patton, William, 218
Paul, Thomas, 286
Paulist Fathers, 164
Pennsylvania Station, 97
Perenyi, Laszlo, 254
Perpendicular Gothic style, 16
pews, 106, 110, 123, 143–44,
    240. *See also* free chapels
Pfeiffer, Carl, 126–28
Phillipson, Emil, 190
Phillips Presbyterian, 236
Pike, James Albert, 215
Pius VII, Pope, 58
Pius X, Pope, 108

Plymouth Baptist Church, 116
Polish, 34
Poole, Thomas Henry, 198, 268
portals, 150
Port Authority Bus
    Terminal, 97, 106, 109
Potter, Edward T., 264
Potter, William A., 194
Pottier & Stymus, 161
Powell, Adam Clayton Jr., 286, 288
Powell, Adam Clayton Sr., 286
Presbyterian churches, 42,
    72, 126, 190, 218, 234, 236
Presbyterians, 72–75, 126–28, 236
Price, Leontyne, 289
Prince of Wales (later
    Edward VII), 19
Proctor, Samuel DeWitt, 288–89
Protestant elites, 140
Provence, France, 150
public schools, 31
Pulitzer, Joseph, 102

Raphael, 172, 175
Rappleyea, Robert, 109
Ravenna, Italy, 164, 263
Reform Judaism synagogues,
    156, 186, 220
Reims Cathedral, 94
Reinhart, Nicholas, 206
Renaissance Revival, 68, 70
Renwick, Aspinwall
    & Russell, 278
Renwick, Henry B., 70
Renwick, James Jr., 8, 68, 70, 76,
    79, 132, 135, 136, 140–42, 143,
    144, 146, 150, 240, 278
Renwick, James Sr., 79
Renwick, William W., 278
Republican Party, 116
reredos, 124
Return Crucifix, 104
Revolutionary War, 14, 23, 28, 72,
    171, 178
    monuments, 27
Riverside Church, 75, 211, 218,
    274
Robertson, R. H., 234, 236
Robeson, Benjamin C., 282–84,
    285
Robeson, Paul, 282
Rockefeller, John D., 75, 211, 218
Rodeph Shalom, 170
Rodin, Auguste, 150
Rogers, James Gamble, 129
Roman basilica style, 83
Romanesque Revival, 54

Romanesque style, 37, 39, 42,
    45, 106, 116, 164, 167, 176, 202,
    221, 234, 240, 254, 256, 274
Romaniote Judaism, 50
Roosevelt, Alice, 84–86
Roosevelt, Eleanor, 135, 242
Roosevelt, Theodore Jr., 129
rose windows, 214, 230
Rourke, Mickey, 109
Rubens, Peter Paul, 125
Ruskin, John, 278
Russian Greek Orthodox
    National Association, 260
Russians, 34, 260
Ryan, Thomas Fortune, 249

saint(s), African American, 31
St. Bartholomew's
    Church, 144, 150–55
St. Catherine of Siena, 226
Saint Denis, Paris, 295
Sainte-Chapelle, Paris, 172
St. Eleftherios Greek
    Orthodox Church, 242
St. Elizabeth of Hungary
    (closed), 253, 254–55
Saint-Gaudens, Augustus, 123, 124
St. George's Church, 84–87
Saint-Gilles-du-Gard,
    Abbey of, 150
St. Ignatius Loyola, 250, 256–59
St. James Church, 242
St. Jean Baptiste Church, 246–49
St. John the Baptist, 94–97, 98, 109
St. John the Divine, Cathedral
    of, 175, 208–13, 295
St. John the Martyr
    (demolished), 8, 234–35
St. Joseph's Church, 64–67
St. Mark's Church-in-
    the-Bowery, 70
St. Mary Grand, 42–45
St. Nicholas of Myra
    Orthodox Church, 68–71
St. Patrick's Cathedral, 8, 56,
    60, 70, 140–49, 150, 164,
    208, 220, 223, 240, 278
    Fair, 143
    funerals, 148
    visitors and tourists, 148
St. Patrick'S Chapel, of Church
    of St. Paul the Apostle, 167
St. Patrick's Old Cathedral/
    Basilica, 8, 56–61
St. Paul's Chapel, 14, 24–27
    Oldest NY Structure, 24
    The Little Chapel That Stood, 26

St. Peter's Church, 28–31, 56–58
St. Peter's Episcopal Church,
    88–91
St. Stephen of Hungary
    (closed), 253, 254–55
St. Thomas Church, 9,
    120–25, 175, 226, 295
St. Thomas More, 263, 268
St. Vincent de Paul Church, 246
Salem United Methodist
    Church, 274–77
sanctuaries
    many purposes of, 10
    origin dates of, 11
San Gennaro (St. Januarius), 56
    festival, 40
San Isidoro y San Leandro
    Western Orthodox Catholic
    Church of Hispanic
    Mozarabic Rite, 260
Santa Croce, Florence, 164
Satterlee, Herbert, 86
Scalabrini Fathers, 40
Schickel, William, 226
Schickel & Ditmars, 40, 253, 256
Schneider, Walter S., 190
Schneider and Herter, 230
Schneier, Arthur, 230–33
Schuyler, Montgomery, 182, 264
Schwab, L. H., 290
Schwarzkopf, Leopold, 156
Scorsese, Martin, 58
Semitic style, 190
September 11 terrorist attack
    (9/11), 19, 26–27, 31, 101, 149
    Out of the Dust exhibit, 27
    responses to, 19
Serracino, Nicholas, 246, 249
Seton, Elizabeth Ann, 60
Shaar Hashomayim, 159
Shire, Edward I., 202
Shoemaker, Samuel Moor, 132
Shrine and Parish Church of
    the Holy Innocents, 102–5
Shrine Church of the Most
    Precious Blood, 40–41
Sisters of Charity, 59
Sleepers (book and movie), 119
Slovaks, 260
Smith, Bernard, 142
Smith, James W., 91
Smith, Kiki, 39
Smith, Oliver, 225
Smith, W. Wheeler, 264
socialism, 136
Spain, 31
Spellman, Francis, 144

stained glass windows, 16, 39, 56, 64, 83, 125, 146, 164, 167, 175, 194, 198, 229, 249, 253, 267, 285
Stein, Clarence S., 223
Steinback, Gustave, 172
Stuyvesant, Peter, 70, 84, 168
Synagogue Rescue Project, 39
synagogues, number of, 171
Szendy, Emil J., 254, 260

Tamid: The Downtown Synagogue, 27
Tammany Hall, 116
Taylor, Billy, 289
Taylor, Matthew A., 172
Taylor, Thomas House, 76, 79
Temple Beth-El, 223
Temple Emanu-El, 220–25
Tenderloin District, 98, 102
theater district, 109
Thomas, Thomas, 31
Thompson, Holmes and Converse, 242
Tiffany, Louis Comfort, 194, 225
Tiffany studio, 83, 176, 194, 197
Times Square, 9, 106, 109, 110, 115
Toussaint, Pierre, 31, 59–60
Tractarians, 110
Treanor, John, 250
Trinity Church, 14–19
    Farm of, 30
    first edifice, burned, 14
    graveyard, 19
    patrons, 16
    Protestant Corporation of, 30
    second edifice, 14–16

third edifice, 16
uptown cemetery, 290
visitors to, 19
Trusteeism, 94
trustees, rule of, 94
Truth, Sojourner, 23, 282
Tubman, Harriet, 282
Tudor Gothic, 286
Tutu, Desmond, 215
twelve-step program, 132

Underground Railroad, 49, 284
United Synagogue of America, 205
University Place Church, 75
Upjohn, Richard, 16, 123
urban renewal, 201

Vallejo, José, 31
Vanderbilt, Alice Gwynne, 150
Vanderbilt, Cornelius, 150
Vanderbilt, William, 150
Vanicky, John, 68
Varela y Morales, Félix, 31, 32
Varick, James, 282
Varick, Richard, 126
Venetian Renaissance, 102
Vesey, William, 14
Victorian Gothic, 126, 218, 236, 290
Victory Chapel, 108–9
Vislocky, John, 68
Vleeshal, Haarlem, Netherlands, 176

Washburn, Edward, 134

Washburn, Emelyn, 134
Washington, George, 14, 24–26, 178
Washington Heights, 290
waterfront, 80
Watts, André, 289
Wells, Joseph C., 75
Welsch, Samuel, 156
Wesley, John, 20
Wesley Chapel, 20
West End Collegiate Church, 176–77
West Side Urban Renewal Plan, 201
Wharton, Edith, 134
Whelan, Father, 28–30
White, Stanford, 150, 164, 167
Wigger, Winand M., 98
Wild, Joseph, 98
Wilde, Robert, 64
Willard, Simeon, 84
William III, 14
Williams, Peter, 23, 282
Wills and Dudley, 120
Winter, Lumen Martin, 164, 167
Wise, Aaron, 186
Wolcott, Oliver Jr., 126
Wolfe, Gerard R., 37, 39
women in churches, as singers, 147
women's gallery, 50

Yorkville, 246, 250, 254, 256, 268

Zion Episcopal Church, 32

PHOTO CREDITS

Front cover: St. Thomas Church (1 West 53rd Street), reredos and altar. See p. 120.
Back cover: Central Synagogue (652 Lexington Avenue), altar. See p. 158.
Spine (top): Church of St. Mary the Virgin (145 West 46th Street), window detail. See p. 113.
Spine (bottom): Eldridge Street Synagogue (12 Eldridge Street), window detail. See p. 36.
p. 2: Temple Emanu-El (1 East 65th Street), main sanctuary. See p. 221.
pp. 12–13: Eldridge Street Synagogue (12 Eldridge Street), main sanctuary
pp. 62–63: Church of St. Francis Xavier (46 West 16th Street), ceiling in the main sanctuary
pp. 92–93: Church of St. Mary the Virgin (145 West 46th Street), apse in the main sanctuary
pp. 130–31: Central Synagogue (652 Lexington Avenue), main sanctuary
pp. 162–63: Advent Lutheran Church (2504 Broadway), reredos
pp. 216–17: Our Lady of Good Counsel (230 East 90th Street), main sanctuary
pp. 272–73: Mother African Methodist Episcopal Zion Church (140–148 West 137th Street), main sanctuary

Project editor: Lauren Bucca
Copy editor: Stephanie Baker
Proofreader: Jennifer Dixon
Production director: Louise Kurtz
Designers: Misha Beletsky and Michael Russem
Maps: Ada Rodriguez

First edition
10 9 8 7 6 5 4 3 2

Library of Congress Cataloging-in-Publication Data

Names: Horowitz, Michael L. 1952– photographer. | Hartman, Elizabeth Anne,
    author.
Title: Divine New York : inside the historic churches and synagogues of
    Manhattan / photographs by Michael L. Horowitz; text by Elizabeth Anne
    Hartman.
Description: [New York] : [Abbeville Press Publishers], [2022] | Includes
    bibliographical references and index. | Summary: "Photographs of the
    interiors of New York City's churches and synagogues"—Provided by
    publisher.
Identifiers: LCCN 2022024492 | ISBN 9780789214454 (hardcover)
Subjects: LCSH: Church architecture–New York (State)—New York—Pictorial
    works. | Synagogue architecture–New York (State)—New York—Pictorial
    works. | Interior architecture–New York (State)—New York—Pictorial
    works. | Manhattan (New York, N.Y.)—Buildings, structures,
    etc.—Pictorial works. | New York (N.Y.)—Buildings, structures,
    etc.–Pictorial works.
Classification: LCC NA5235.N6 H67 2022 | DDC 726.09747/1–dc23/eng/20220712
LC record available at https://lccn.loc.gov/2022024492

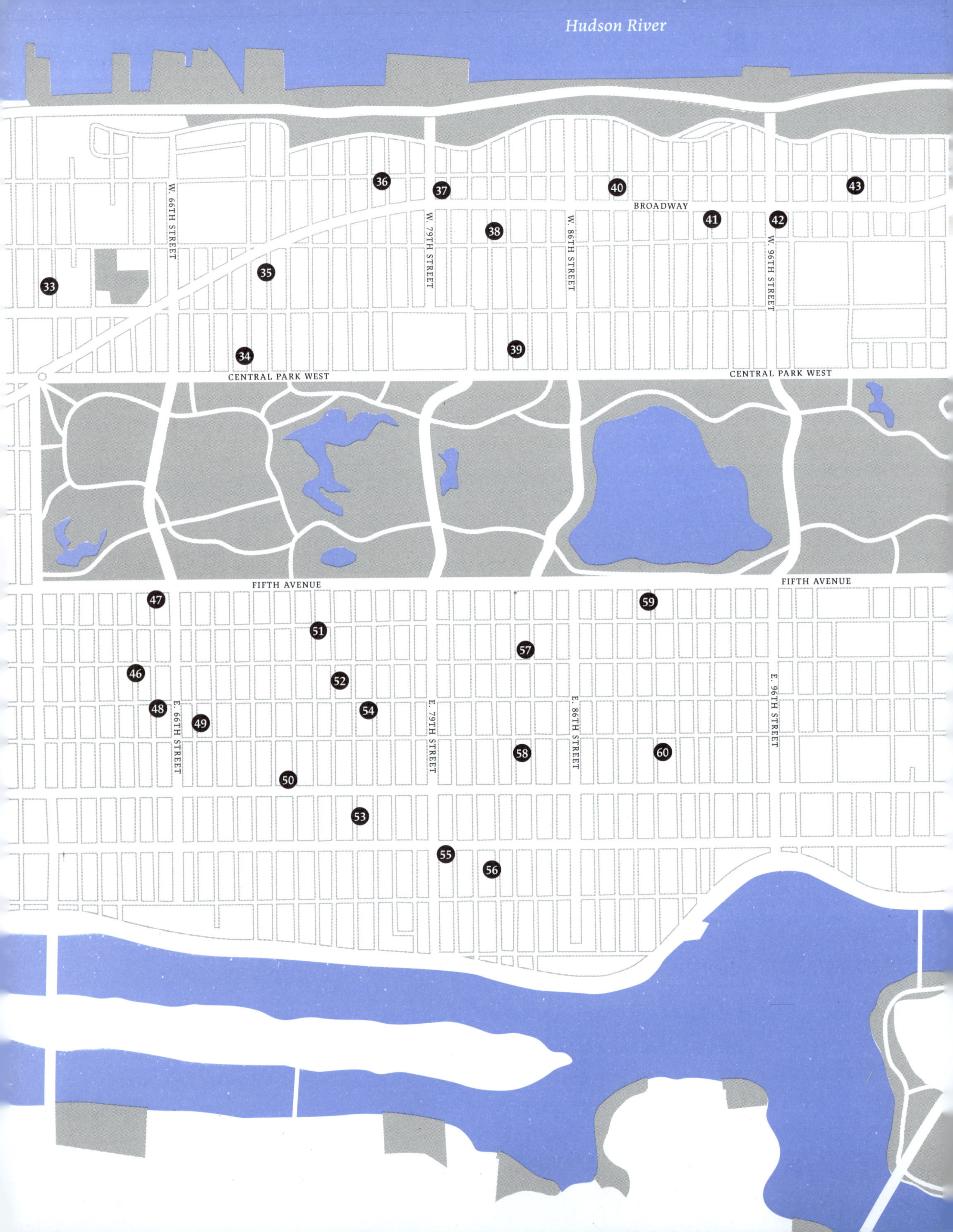

Hudson River
W. 66TH STREET
W. 79TH STREET
W. 86TH STREET
W. 96TH STREET
BROADWAY
CENTRAL PARK WEST
CENTRAL PARK WEST
FIFTH AVENUE
FIFTH AVENUE
E. 66TH STREET
E. 79TH STREET
E. 86TH STREET
E. 96TH STREET
33
34
35
36
37
38
39
40
41
42
43
46
47
48
49
50
51
52
53
54
55
56
57
58
59
60